REMEMBERING TO LIVE

LESSONS I LEARNED CRAWLING OUT OF HELL

Khalil Rafati

with
Jeremy Brown

REMEMBERING TO LIVE

978-1-7349642-0-2 (Paperback) | 978-1-7349642-1-9 (eBook)

TABLE OF CONTENTS

MEDICAL DISCLAIMER

The information provided in this book is designed to provide helpful information on the subjects discussed. This book is not meant to be used, nor should it be used, to diagnose or treat any medical condition.

For diagnosis or treatment of any medical problem, consult your healthcare provider. The publisher and author are not responsible for any specific health or allergy needs that may require medical supervision and are not liable for any damages or negative consequences from any treatment, action, application, or preparation to any person reading or following the information in this book.

References are provided for informational purposes only and do not constitute endorsement of any websites or other sources.

Readers should be aware that the websites listed in this book may change.

INTRODUCTION

I'm a complicated, flawed, and deeply wounded individual. It took me many years and countless trials and tribulations to come to this realization.

I behaved carelessly throughout my teens and twenties, and unfortunately, even into my early thirties. My only concern in life was satisfying my needs and wants, without consideration for others or any sign of a moral compass.

I got sober when I was 33 years old. At that time I was homeless, addicted to crack and heroin, my teeth were falling out of my head...I was a walking corpse.

And here I am, now.

My story seems to resonate with a lot of people. When my first book, *I Forgot to Die*, came out in 2015 I began getting messages every single day from people all over the world. Soon after, it was translated into four languages to reach even more people.

The vast majority of messages I get from readers are about how my story has impacted their lives in a positive way. I keep all of these messages and respond to as many of them as I can. But there have been a few complaints about how the end of the first book felt rushed.

And to be honest with you...it was.

Toward the end of writing *I Forgot to Die*, I began to doubt myself. I questioned whether anybody was ever going to read the book. I got scared. So I panicked, and I raced through the end of my story just to get it done and out of my head.

This has left some people with the impression that I became sober, and the next day I was a millionaire living the life of Riley. As you'll see in this book, that is not the case.

I hope these pages will resonate with you and bring something beneficial to your life.

—Khalil,
October 25th, 2019

PREFACE: REMEMBER TO LIVE

Put your phone down and get away from it.

Get away from your computer and the internet and your Bitcoin and your Dow Jones Industrial Average.

Stop watching the non-stop news cycle. It's all a con. It's all a hustle.

Get as far away from electronics as possible and go find your stream. Find your pond, find your lake or ocean and sit and be still.

Listen to the wind.

Listen to the mountains, listen to the waves of the ocean, listen to the stream and listen to the birds. They know everything.

Go to bed with the sun, sleep with the moon, and wake up with the sun again.

Hug your children every time you see them and every time you leave them. Play with them, no matter how old they are. Show them you love them.

Tell your partner that you love them. Look them in the eye and take a deep breath and tell them they are the most important thing in the world to you.

Go sweat, go get muddy. Ride a bicycle, go feel what it's like. Feel what it's like to sprint as fast as you can for as long as you can.

Do some yoga, or stretching, every day, even if it's just for ten minutes.

Gather every gift card you have in your possession. Put them in an envelope and give them to one person who is less fortunate than you.

Gather all of your credit card points and frequent flier miles and loose change you've been saving in jars and take that dream vacation you've always fantasized about.

The next time you go out to eat, pick a random couple or family at the restaurant. Very discreetly, without them knowing or finding out, pay for their entire meal including a twenty percent tip. It's not that difficult. Just ask your server.

Pick up trash when you see it on the ground and don't look around to see if anyone notices.

Return your shopping cart to the front of the store regardless of the weather, and again, do not look around and see if anyone notices.

At least once, more if you can afford it, tip a housekeeper or a bus boy one hundred dollars and get out of there before they realize how much money you left. Don't do it somewhere you always go—make sure it's a stranger you'll likely never see again.

It's never too late or too soon to accomplish your dreams.

Too old is not an excuse.

Not enough time is not an excuse.

Lack of skills or resources is not an excuse.

I am proof of that. I can't spell or type but my dream of writing a bestselling book came true and lots of other dreams too. I was 45 when I wrote it.

Stop spiraling on your phone, social media, reality TV, and start walking towards your dreams.

Execute a spending freeze. Stop spending money you don't have and attention you can't spare on bullshit that doesn't matter. You'll be amazed at how much you can accomplish in 18 hours a day with clear intentions and few distractions.

Or look back 10 years from now and say, "I should've...I could've..."

The goal is to live a happy life, but the goal should also be to have a happy death. To die with a smile on your face knowing you have given life your best effort and have been the man or woman God intended you to be.

One of my biggest fears when I was younger was looking back at my life and being full of regrets. For not realizing and achieving my full potential. The thought made me shudder!

This is it, we only get one life.

Most people are asleep.

Most people delude themselves into thinking this is a dress rehearsal.

It's not.

It's right here, right now!

Write down your dreams and your goals and go get them!

There are two types of people on this planet: People who talk about things and people who do things.

Who do you want to be?

What do you want to do?

BECAUSE YOU CAN BE AND DO WHATEVER YOU WANT!

If an idiot like me, seemingly born to lose with no talent, no skill, and no education can succeed, then anyone can.

We will blink and this will all be over someday.

Maybe sooner than we think.

This is your life, no one else's, so live it as if your opinion is the one that truly matters.

Be kind to everyone you meet, smile at people even if they don't smile back.

Always leave a good tip even if the service is horrible. They need it more than you do.

Call your mom and tell her you love her, some day she won't be in this realm anymore. If she's not here anymore know that she's still very much with you and loves you no matter what and always will!

Thank God for each day, each meal, each moment—whatever "God" means to you.

And speaking of meals—if you're on vacation or having a really tough day, ignore everything I say in this book about healthy eating and throw all dietary restrictions out the window. They don't call it comfort food for nothing. Don't worry, your green juice, butter/oil coffee, intermittent fasting, gluten intolerance, ancestral, carnivore, macrobiotic, paleo, primal, vegan, and raw food diets will be waiting for you with open arms.

Anything is possible if you put your mind to it. But your mind must be clean. Meaning, if you have any type of consistent drug or alcohol use, it must be eliminated.

I'm not talking about the occasional glass of wine with dinner or cannabis use, but even with minimal use, the substances are still toxins. They will still slow you down and cloud your mind.

If you want the amazing benefits of red wine, order yourself a bottle of resveratrol.

If you want the amazing benefits of cannabis, order a bottle of CBD oil. It is derived from the hemp plant and has no psychoactive effects.

With these, you can have your cake and eat it too.

Bottom line, I promise you, if you eliminate these toxins from your body you will expedite the process of realizing your dreams.

But even more important than detoxing your mind: it must be free from resentment or blaming others.

Your thoughts must be kind and loving to rejoin the life force that is ever present, ever flowing and unlimited.

Be Here Now means exactly that.

Be present, be conscious, WAKE UP!

You can do ANYTHING!

Life is so short.

Remember to live.

A COMPLETELY TRANSPARENT TIMELINE FROM ZERO TO HERO

When I was living at New Perceptions, which was a transitional living house also known as a halfway house, I was given $40 a week by the Musicians Assistance Program, or MAP. I was 33 years old and somehow managed to live off of less than $6 a day, and that included daily cigarettes. I'm still very good friends with my housemate Frank Humphries (AKA Frankie Violence), and we often reminisce about those times. We drank a lot of tap water and lived mostly off of noodles and industrial-sized jars of Prego tomato sauce topped with tons of hot sauce.

There was some bizarre no-name gas station up the street from our house, and they had this super cheap generic tobacco. So we would buy the tobacco and rolling papers and roll our own cigarettes. I know it sounds disgusting, but I have to be honest with you—it was one of the most amazing times of my life. I have never, and will probably never again, laugh as much and as hard as I did during those few months. Jacked up on ridiculously strong coffee and the rush of those cheap handmade filterless cigarettes, we laughed and told stories and viciously made fun of one another.

Every now and then someone's feelings got hurt and we would of course back off, but the moment the dust settled we would go right back to attacking one another. Race and sexual orientation were typically the basis of our jokes, but it didn't stop there. Because I was a singer, they made fun of my voice. Frank played guitar, so we tore apart his guitar playing.

But nothing was off the table: Mothers, penis size, talent or lack thereof, etc. I laughed so hard it was common to wake up with sore abdominal muscles, as if I had done a thousand sit-ups the night before. I'm laughing now just thinking about it! Penniless, broken, and without hope we laughed so deep and so hard our pain and suffering was transformed into camaraderie, community, fortitude and strength.

Bob Forrest, who had been a counselor to all of us at the Pasadena Recovery Center, loved to call us the House of Losers. We were the worst of the worst. The worst drug addicts and the worst behaved, and nobody knew what to do with us.

The cool kids, the smart ones, the ones with real talent or fame were all sent to a famous sober living house in West L.A. called Genesis House. Shit, it even had a cool name! But we weren't allowed to go there out of fear that we would bring the entire house down by relapsing or starting fights. When it comes to new sobriety, it only takes one bad apple to spoil the whole bunch, and our house was a bushel of bad apples.

Bob's philosophy was to take all of the bad apples and quarantine them, which resulted in our House of Losers. I fit right in. I was a 33-year-old ex-junkie high school dropout, convicted felon with no talent, no resume, and no hope.

At least, that's how I seemed on the outside.

On the inside, I had started to build a personal relationship with a God of my own understanding.

Not my dad's God or atheistic belief system.

Not my mom's God.

And most definitely not the punishing God I was taught about in grade school.

No, I'm talking about my own God. My relationship with that God had started many, many years earlier as a child, but had always been interrupted by what I saw and experienced. I always felt in my heart that there was a God, but because of what I went through, I came to believe that that God did not love me or care about me.

Bottoming out—I mean **truly** bottoming out—is a very bizarre experience. I don't mean troubles and hardships, because everybody goes through those all the time. But truly bottoming out and losing everything and not having any options brings you to your knees and gives you absolute clarity. Well, my absolute clarity at 33 years old was that I had made a complete fucking mess of my life and God loving me or not loving me had absolutely zero to do with it.

God created me and gave me life, but God also gave me free will. I took that free will and went off the rails, selfishly seeking comfort and pleasure at all costs. I eventually got to the point where I didn't give a shit who I hurt. I don't mean physically—I was never a tough or violent guy, but the pain I put my mother, ex-girlfriends, and my friends through...oh man. They probably would have preferred violence over the mind games, cheating, and outright manipulation.

So there I was, 33 years old, literally on my knees during my second day in rehab. I was crying, accepting the fact that there was no one to blame except myself. Oh my God, I was so empty. I had nothing.

But again, the strange thing about bottoming out and having nothing is the clarity and humility I began to experience. Humility is the most underrated supernatural power one can possess, and very few of us ever truly embrace it.

With humility came faith. And hope. True faith and hope that if I stayed humble and never stopped working toward being the man God intended me to be, I would be okay.

If you saw me today, you might think, "Damn, faith and hope made that dude a millionaire?"

Yes, and no. I didn't just pray, hope for the best, and roll out of my halfway house bunk and fall into success.

It's the "never stopped working" part that made me a millionaire. Faith and hope kept me going when it seemed like the work might kill me.

My first job after sobriety was painting walls, carrying sheetrock, and removing tree stumps for $10 an hour.

After one week I picked up a second job when a woman named Sherman who owns a dog grooming business named Sherman's Place hired me to wash dogs. The incredible Louis Gossett Jr. was dropping his dogs off one day and struck up a conversation with me. When he realized how down on my luck I was, he hired me to walk his two beautiful dogs every day and was kind enough to pay me $500 a month, which was a massive amount of money for me at the time.

Then another customer, Pietra, came in and hired me to walk her dogs. She had two incredible young sons who took a liking to me, and she ended up also hiring me to teach them how to boogie board out in front of their house. On top of that, I reached out to some of my old car detailing clients and got work from them.

I made an arrangement with my sponsor Robbie and his wife Laurie to live in their house rent free in exchange for washing their cars and dogs and running errands.

I got a job at a rehab facility called Malibu Ranch, working the night shift. About six months after that I got an additional job at another rehab owned by Fred Segal called The Canyon. At this point I was working around the clock at the two rehab centers and still managing to walk all the dogs and serve as a "manny" for the boogie boarding boys.

Then Cindy Landon, the beautiful widow of Michael Landon, befriended me and also gave me work running errands. Cindy has this amazing spiritual glow to her. She's very active in various charities and wants to save all of the animals...which might explain why she invited me to dinner for my birthday.

She took me to Taverna Tony, a wonderful Greek restaurant in Malibu, and we were having a great time when this six-foot-six, incredibly menacing guy sat down at the table with us. Cindy introduced him as her business manager, Dennis. The contrast between them was startling. Cindy was an angel, and Dennis looked like a straight-up gangster. He was gruff and blunt, cursing like a sailor. But he was a perfect fit for his job, which was to protect Cindy.

I was nervous to begin with—hell, I was always nervous back then—but Dennis' presence made me even moreso. I felt tremendous relief when we were done eating. Cindy got up to leave and I moved to follow, but Dennis said, "Khalil, stick around. We need to talk."

I looked to Cindy for help, but she seemed to think everything was fine. I felt like I might never see her again.

When she was gone, Dennis said, "Look kid, for whatever reason Cindy really likes you. She wants me to reassure you that if anybody tries to hurt you, or if you ever need anything, you can call this phone number."

He handed me a card with a number on it. It was an 818 number, and to this day I still have it memorized. Then he handed me an envelope.

"Open it," he said.

I did, but couldn't understand what I was looking at. It was a check for $3,000, made out to me.

Dennis said, "Cindy wants you to have that. She wants you to go out and get some decent clothes and get yourself a laptop."

I said, "No, no, I can't take—"

Dennis slammed his hand on the table. "You shut the fuck up! I'm not asking you, I'm telling you! Take that fucking money and go get yourself some decent clothes. You can't dress like that, people won't take you seriously."

I looked down at my torn, second-hand jeans and the T-shirt that was one size too small. I nodded my head.

"And go get yourself a laptop," Dennis said.

A laptop? I thought. *What am I going to do with a laptop?*

But I just nodded again. Dennis wasn't someone you argued with.

The following day, I was at Cindy's running errands when her assistant Diane handed me a DVD.

"Cindy wants you to watch this," she said.

The DVD was the documentary *The Secret*. I spent a few moments trying to figure out how I was going to watch it, then it hit me: the laptop. A few days later I went shopping for clothes and got myself a laptop, then went home and watched the entire documentary three times in a row.

That was the spark that started the forest fire. I was already reading a lot at that time, mostly the Christian philosopher Emmet Fox and 12-step literature, and I was desperate and hungry for anything positive to put into my head. Within days I purchased the books *Think and Grow Rich*, *Psycho-Cybernetics*, and *The Power of Positive Thinking*. I watched *The Secret* and read and reread those books during every spare moment I had. During my night shifts at the rehab facility I would fall asleep reading, wake up and read some more until I fell asleep again...all night long.

And I saved every penny I made from my half-dozen or so jobs. I never had to spend money on food because both of the rehab facilities had tons of it. The Canyon had organic raw food chefs, and the pantry was always stocked with tons of organic snacks and vegetables.

Every time I got paid I would rush to Bank of America and cash my check, then race to Inglewood to buy rare gold coins. Why was I buying gold coins? Because a guy named Peter—who I met in a 12-step program—was a gold bug, and he told me gold was going to go parabolic over the next few years when the economy collapsed.

That information terrified the hell out of me, but also inspired me. He assured me that if I bought these rare old gold coins, not only would they be worth a lot more within a short period of time, but because they had been minted before 1933 there was some strange tax loophole that allowed me to pay no taxes on them.

And just like Peter said, the economy ultimately collapsed two years later and the value of those gold coins went through the roof.

Thanks to the laptop from Cindy, I had also started taking online classes to get my Certified Alcohol Drug Counselor Associate license, and I started taking weekend courses to become a Certified Interventionist. I started doing interventions on the side and rather than getting paid $14 an hour at the rehab facilities, I got $5,000 for one weekend of work.

I ended up getting fired from The Canyon and began doing more interventions, as well as sober companion gigs. Sober companions work one-on-one with someone who is newly sober to help them stay the course. My first job as a sober companion went great. Then came my second opportunity, and things got weird.

The person looking to hire me sent an email asking me to send an invoice and explain my fees. I didn't know how to reply to an email, so I asked Robbie for help. He sat down at the computer and began to type.

"How much do you want to charge?" he asked me.

"I charged $200 a day last time, but I heard that some companies are getting up to $1,000 a day. So...$400?"

Robbie said, "Okay, $800."

"No no, wait!"

"Relax," Robbie said, and hit Send.

I couldn't believe it. Robbie had told my new potential client I charged $800 a day, which they would never pay. I was screwed. I'd never hear from them again, unless it was to laugh at me and tell me to go to hell.

The response came back immediately:

"Does that include expenses?"

Robbie was laughing his ass off. He started typing again.

I tried to see the screen. "What are you telling them?"

His reply said, "No, the fee is $800 a day plus expenses."

"Robbie, no!"

Send.

"Robbie, what the hell?!"

Again, the response came back immediately:

"Please provide a mailing address where we can send the check."

"Holy shit," I said. "They're actually going to pay me $800 a day."

Robbie said, "Yeah, plus expenses, and they're going to pay you up-front for the month. I put that in there too."

"*What?*"

Robbie just smiled.

That was the day I learned the incredible lesson that it was my responsibility to establish my time and skills as highly valuable commodities. I had thought it was the opposite—if I set my prices too high, no one would hire me.

Robbie explained that it was actually the opposite. If I had told these people my fee was $200 or even $400 a day, they would have said, "We'll get back to you," and I'd never hear from them again. I wouldn't be establishing my value. If I wasn't worth more money, I wasn't worth their time.

I continued my sober companion jobs and buying my gold. And when the bottom dropped out of the U.S. economy and house values began to plummet, Robbie's wife Laurie wanted to sell the house. Robbie disagreed; he wanted to keep it until the value rose again and rent it out in the meantime. It became a real point of contention between the two of them.

By that time I was so beat up from traveling around the world, babysitting drug addicts and alcoholics, I started mapping out a plan to open my own transitional living facility. Letting the clients come to me seemed very attractive, and there were only two sober living houses in Malibu at that time, and both of them were dumps.

During one of the heated Robbie and Laurie debates about renting vs. selling, I boldly and naïvely stepped in and said, "Why don't you let me rent the house? I can run my transitional living here."

And to my great surprise, Laurie said, "Okay, but I want you to fix up the house and paint it."

I said, "Are you serious? You're willing to let me rent the house?"

"Yes," she said.

From there it all happened very quickly. They found a house they loved in Venice and moved out, and on a shoestring and a prayer I got started. I painted and fixed up the whole place with a couple of friends. I bought some tools and did an insane amount of landscaping and tree trimming.

I hired an energy expert who was referred to me by Premier Research Labs, and we transformed the energy of the estate by placing crystals and hematite in thirty different locations around the property. We also mixed decomposed granite into the soil and did a bunch of other really wacky, woo-woo things to the house and property. When it was ready, I opened Riviera Recovery in a multi-million dollar home on the Pacific coast.

The place was an immediate success. I had a waiting list within the first month of opening.

I continued doing sober companion jobs and continued to watch the value of my gold and silver coins rise. I never relaxed.

There were lots of ups and downs. Lots of failures. I got burned more times than I care to remember. I loaned money to people and never got paid back. I invested almost every penny I had in a business with a friend and never saw that money again.

But I kept working, I kept saving, and I kept succeeding. While people were out surfing or having social lives I worked seven days a week, 16 to 18 hours a day. If I lost a bunch of money on something stupid I would make a bunch more.

I just kept going. My physical health suffered. My relationships definitely suffered. I didn't realize how overworked and miserable I was.

I just kept going.

In 2010 I made another very risky decision. I signed the lease on a 1200-square-foot commercial space to open up my very own juice bar. I had been going to juice bars every single day, some of them local and some spread out all over L.A. I was obsessed with smoothies and juices. I loved the energy they gave me, and I was watching miracles happen at Riviera Recovery when I made them for my clients.

When I made the decision to open up a juice bar, I signed the lease without even having a lawyer look at it. Then, once again, I got to work. After a lot of sweat, swearing, praying, faith, and hope, eleven months later we opened the doors of our first SunLife Organics location.

As I write this, we have fourteen locations.

What happened between that first location and now?

That story must be told, but it's not in this book. This book is about Change, with a capital "C", and how to make it happen in your life. The saga of SunLife certainly has Change in it, and its lessons are instructive, but most of them are not repeatable. It would be impossible to take the audacity, serendipity, and pure insanity of how SunLife grew and apply it to your life or business.

But again, that's a story for another book…

My goal with this book is to help you change. To find and fulfill your purpose and potential.

The good news is, you don't have to be a high school dropout, former drug addict, and convicted felon to change.

You just need to have the willingness, humility, and faith to just keep going until you get there.

THE INTOXICATION OF A PERFECT EXISTENCE

You are reading this book because you want to **change**.

There is something inside you pushing and driving to take the next step toward your true potential.

Maybe that step is finally being honest with yourself about what you're putting in and on your body.

You know, the stuff labeled as food, beverages, and cosmetics, but is actually **poison**.

Maybe it's quitting the job that is slowly killing you and robbing the rest of the world of your true talent and purpose.

Maybe it's the drink and the drug and the lower companions who want you to stay high—just like them—and finally getting help so you don't die today.

Or maybe…

Maybe that step is just accepting the absolute, concrete, amazing fact that you **can change**.

Because you can.

Notice I did not say you are reading this book because you ***NEED*** to change.

There are countless people who need to change but don't want to.

Right now, someone is shooting up, or anesthetizing themselves with another fast food burger, or seeking fake and empty attention on social media instead of connecting with another real person. Hell, there are probably a few overachievers doing all of these at once!

But here's the thing: It doesn't matter what I, you, or anyone else **thinks** or **says** when it comes to someone else changing.

When I was getting drunk and high every day and someone told me I needed to stop, my reaction was, "Fuck you, I'm gonna do twice as much now."

They were right, of course.

I did need to stop.

I needed to change.

But none of that mattered because I didn't **want** to change.

Getting high felt amazing to me at the time. Self-medicating with crack, heroin and cocaine filled a massive, bottomless hole inside me.

It was the only way I could feel whole, **alive**.

Of course, I **told** people I wanted to quit drugs and get sober. In fact, it is a hallmark characteristic of any hardcore drug addict—all they ever talk about is wanting to get clean or wanting to get high. I wouldn't shut up about it.

I tried outpatient, Subutex, and Buprenex. I tried cold turkey. I tried only doing heroin because cocaine was the problem. I tried only doing cocaine because heroin was the problem. I went on methadone and woke up every morning at 5 AM and drove to Pontius Avenue in West L.A. and stood in line at the methadone clinic.

I did that for months. Every time I see a commercial for *The Walking Dead* I get the shivers because it reminds me what it was like being on methadone maintenance.

I literally tried everything, but deep down I still **wanted** the drugs and alcohol and how they made me feel more than I **wanted** to be clean.

I had to hit rock bottom before I truly **wanted** to change.

Actually, I had to hit rock bottom then grab a pick and shovel and dig even deeper with my bare hands until I had nothing left in me. No will to continue. I went until the wheels fell off. I continued until I was a rotting corpse with my teeth falling out of my head.

In that hopeless state of despair, at one hundred and nine pounds and open abscesses covering my arms, legs, chest, and face, I finally found the humility to be honest with myself and concede to my innermost self that I was in fact a drug addict and an alcoholic and that I had to change.

Only then was I ready to change.

Maybe you're there right now.

Maybe you can see it coming and it scares you to death.

Either way, believe me when I say: That is good.

Change is **terrifying**.

Change is **uncomfortable**.

Are you uncomfortable yet?

I hope so.

Comfort makes us cowards.

Comfort is the enemy.

Constantly seeking comfort can rob you of your soul without your consent.

If you are comfortable, you are not changing.

I am living proof that change has the power to bring you everything you want.

If you are ready, willing, and want to change, you can and will have an incredible life full of joy and deep meaning.

Who the Hell Am I?

32 years old	48 years old
109 lbs	161 lbs
Homeless	Healthy and prosperous
Miserable	Happy
Teeth falling out	Beautiful smile
Doing drugs all night	In bed by 9:30
Self-obsessed	Driven to help others
Addicted to cocaine, heroin, and crack	Addicted to feeling amazing and being the person I was intended and deserve to be

Before we dive in, let's address the big question: Why should you give a damn what I say?

I mean, I'm not a doctor.

I'm not a scientist or a nutritionist.

I'm not a guru or mystic.

I can be shallow and narcissistic.

I'm a show-off.

I am still, at times, a sad little boy stuck inside an adult body, desperate for attention and validation.

I make a dozen mistakes a day, on a good day.

So why should you listen to me?

Here's why:

In 2002 I was homeless and addicted to crack, cocaine, and heroin.

I was unemployed and unemployable.

My teeth were falling out of my head and my body was rotting from the inside out.

I weighed 109 pounds and had a staph infection, ringworm, and scabies.

I looked like a walking corpse.

I **wanted** to die.

And, because I have a relentless drive to get what I want—both good and bad—I actually succeeded.

I intentionally overdosed on heroin and flatlined. I clearly recall leaving my body and looking down at it while the paramedics hit me with a defibrillator, again and again, until I flew back into my body and opened my eyes. I'm only here today because of their amazing work.

But as crazy as it sounds, even after overdosing and flatlining, I still hadn't hit rock bottom. I checked myself out of the hospital and continued to get high, sharing needles with other addicts—some of them with full-blown AIDS—and getting into catastrophic car accidents that should have killed me again, for good.

This is how rock bottom looked for me when I finally smashed into it: I overdosed on pure cocaine and ended up partially blind and temporarily paralyzed from the waist down in a gully, where I buried myself in dirt and leaves to avoid the police scouring the area for me.

Bugs crawled on my face and into my ears and I couldn't do anything to stop them. Even if I could have, I didn't want to. I deserved to die and rot right there.

My own mother wouldn't take my phone calls anymore.

Shit, my *coke dealer* wouldn't even take my calls.

In that moment I surrendered. I gave myself up to whatever higher power would listen and begged for this nightmare to end, one way or another:

"God, please, please, please. I don't want to do this anymore. I can't do this anymore. Please just let me see again, please let me walk again, please don't let me go to jail. I swear I will never drink or get high again. Please just let me get out of this and let me get my vision back and let me be able to walk again and I will never ever do it again."

But unlike all the other times I'd sworn I was done, that time—I meant it.

Laying in that ditch, blind and paralyzed with bugs crawling on me, I knew it was all my fault. I was the only one to blame. And I decided right then and there that if I allowed myself to continue living that way—if you could even call it living—I'd rather die and let the dirt have me.

I finally **wanted** to change.

So I reached out for help.

I met some kind and loving people who showed me that there was a way out. I learned how to eat and drink healing foods.

I learned about having a higher power, something greater than myself.

I learned how to augment my foods with state-of-the-art supplements, vitamins, and minerals. I bought hundreds of books on self-help/personal development. I watched countless documentaries and listened to a million different podcasts.

I learned how to exercise and reap the benefits of yoga, meditation, prayer, journaling, and sauna.

I started three successful businesses, including SunLife Organics, which now has fourteen locations and is growing fast.

I wrote a book and found happiness and meaning in my life.

So again, why should you listen to me?

Because I want to share everything I learned on the road from a living hell to a life beyond my wildest dreams.

I don't know what you're struggling with. It might be alcoholism or drug problems. It might be overeating or overspending. It might be gambling, love and sex addiction, depression, self-sabotaging behaviors, or anxiety.

It might be all of the above.

I am here, completely open and vulnerable. I am a normal person. Shit, that's not even true. I am a person who had a lot of cards stacked against me, lacking any real skill or talent.

But I am a living example that you can get better.

You can regain your health and happiness and achieve success and abundance.

YOU CAN CHANGE.

My goal with *Remembering to Live* is to help you use the incredible power of

change to overcome—and *recover* from—whatever is keeping you from reaching your full potential.

As you read this book and start to make changes in your life, you may hit a point where you feel stuck, unsure, like you can't go on.

Like it isn't worth it.

Like **you** aren't worth it.

Please remember:

It is.

You are.

Are you ready to listen?

Good.

Let's get started.

"Character, like a photograph, develops in darkness."

— YOUSUF KARSH

DO YOU WANT TO CHANGE?

You Are Getting Exactly What You Want from Life

Do you want to change?

Or do you want to **talk** about changing?

Because here's the truth:

You Are Getting Exactly What You Want from Life

Do You Want to be Saved?

Do you want to **change**?

Or do you want to be **saved**?

Because this book **will not** save you.

ONLY YOU WILL SAVE YOU.

You Have to Want to Change

Most people do not want to change.

Most people just want their toys back.

Their girlfriend back, their boyfriend back, their spouse back, even though they mistreated them and would continue to do so.

Most people wish they hadn't been caught because that is forcing them to pretend to change. To build a facade.

Most people want money so they can afford not to change.

Most people just want someone to listen to their sad story and tell them they don't need to change.

If you are reading this and truly want to change, you absolutely can. And I can help you.

But you have to be absolutely clear on how you want to change.

"I want to be rich."

Why? Then what? Will you keep doing the shitty habits that are keeping you from being rich right now?

Rich does not solve problems. In fact, it often creates a lot more of them.

Money solves problems. But rich just amplifies who and what you already are. If you're a shithead and you become rich, you'll just be an even bigger shithead.

And what does rich mean to you? Never being hungry again? The unconditional love of your family? Sitting on the helipad of your yacht sipping champagne out of fresh coconuts while you sail around the world livestreaming on social media?

We'll get into the whole money and happiness thing later. Because nothing else matters if you don't truly want to change and are willing to do so.

If you're deluding yourself into believing you want to change, if you're only seeking comfort or someone to provide a magic pill, I'm not your guy and this is not the book for you.

Not until you're ready.

"There is nothing in a caterpillar that tells you it's going to be a butterfly."

—R. BUCKMINSTER FULLER

You Can Only Change Yourself

No one else can change you.

You can't change anyone else.

If you are reading this because of someone else who needs to change, the first thing you need to know is that you did not create their behavior. It is not your fault.

They can get their own copy—this one is for you.

Your weapons of choice will not work against someone else's dragons.

At the end of the day my job, your job, as human beings is to serve, not save. There is only one savior.

We used to grind it out in that tiny little town I'm from in Ohio. Godless winters so cold and dark they'd break our souls and crush our spirits. And then seemingly out of nowhere, after months of melancholy and despair, spring break would hit.

We'd race down to Florida by Greyhound bus, or if we were lucky by car, driving 24 hours straight doing 80 miles an hour down I-75! Through Kentucky and all its truck stops and wild dogs wandering along the highway. Down through Atlanta where we'd stop off at giant shopping malls to shoplift Ralph Lauren rugby shirts with padded elbows.

Fueled by Doritos, 7-11 hot dogs, Coca-Cola and the promise of girls equally as desperate and disenchanted as us looking for escape from our mundane midwestern existence. We would spend the entire week drunk and blistering in the sun, slathered in baby oil and swimming in cheap beer from sunup to sundown, sharing our bodies and stories and hopes and dreams.

I can't remember what year it was but I was with Chuck Rogers, Todd Byzinski and a few other guys. (One whose sister I was secretly dating, and I was sure he was going to beat me up when Todd wasn't around to protect me.) I spent the whole week sleeping with one eye open.

At some point during that trip I took a solo morning walk on the beach and promised myself I would escape.

I promised myself I would live someplace warm and sunny one day.

I promised myself, standing in the warmth of that beautiful morning sun, that I would forget my awful existence and become somebody new.

My Job

When I was younger I thought my job was to save people. I thought part of that process was some quasi-therapy where we sat around all day sharing sad stories, putting in zero effort to change and complaining about how life was all about floundering and failing.

But once I actually wanted to change my life and worked my ass off toward that change, I started to see the results I'd been whining about for years. It was actually happening. But I still spent time listening to others complain about how unfair it all is, then do absolutely nothing to change. And when I was younger I had time for that. Or thought I did, anyway.

I don't have that time. Nobody does. You don't.

When we started SunLife Organics I thought my job was to make amazing smoothies and juices so people could thrive on real, nutrient-dense food, sometimes for the first time in their lives. Which was true then and still is to this day. Of course, my job was also to wash blenders, plunge toilets, wipe tables, stock shelves, create recipes, hire and fire people, review contracts, high-five everyone, and a million other things.

That is still true today.

But those things aren't my job. They are an amazing, fulfilling opportunity that allows me to do the work I'm truly meant to do.

Help people.

Inspire people.

Show people that they can live their best life.

And I'm not talking about working your ass off at a job you hate, making other people rich while you rack up massive debt so you can sneak away to an all-inclusive beach resort for one week a year. Posting a shot of your feet with some white sand and turquoise water with the caption, "Rough day at the office lol!" or "Life is good!"

LIFE IS GOOD.

IT'S AMAZING.

But that's not life. That's not what we're talking about here.

We're talking about being able to go to that beach every day if you want to. But also, not spending every day thinking about going to that beach because you've fooled yourself into thinking that's the only time you can be happy.

We're talking about making that beach an option, not a requirement.

It's my job, my honor, my privilege to help you get there.

You Like and What You Want Are Two Different Things

I **like** ice cream.

I **want** to look great when I take my shirt off.

Sad and silly that a 50-year-old man cares so much about physical appearance and what others think, especially because dad bods are so in right now. But whatever, I don't have to walk on water to give good advice.

So guess what? Nine times out of ten I skip the ice cream.

Because it doesn't align with what I want.

I used to be embarrassed to take my shirt off. It had a negative impact on my life. I would skip a beach party or swim because I knew it meant I'd be shirtless.

I'd spend the whole party worrying about it instead of enjoying time with friends.

I don't worry about taking my shirt off now, and I am much happier because of it.

This may sound ridiculous.

I mean, does it really matter?

It does to me.

But it's only partially about looking good.

Here's what it's really about:

I want to avoid the pain of feeling embarrassed more than I want the pleasure of eating ice cream.

Or pizza.

Or Doritos. (More on those later…they haunt me.)

There is No Secret

A friend and I met for dinner, and he wanted to jump on some burgers and fries.

I said, "No, come on. I'm treating. I'll take you to this place I know, Porta Via. They have this amazing wild salmon and organic arugula salad."

He looked a little disappointed.

"Come on," I said. "You'll see."

When we got there I ordered the salmon and arugula and he ordered...pasta.

I said, "Pasta? That's no different than the burger and fries."

"No, this is healthy," he said. "And even if it isn't, one meal won't make a difference."

I kept my big mouth shut.

After dinner we walked around the newly-opened Palisades Village. Then we walked past McConnell's, famous for their delicious ice cream.

My friend said, "Oh man, I want some."

He walked inside and checked the flavors.

"What are you going to get?" he asked.

"Nothing," I said.

"No, you bought dinner, this is my treat. Get whatever you want."

"It's fine," I said. "I don't want any. I mean, I love ice cream, but I'm not going to get anything."

"Dude," he said, "this little cup of ice cream doesn't mean anything."

Right then and there, he told me exactly what he **wanted** in life.

Because that little cup of ice cream meant **everything**.

It meant he wanted to follow his **impulses** more than his **habits**.

It meant he wanted to be **unhealthy** and **out of shape** more than he wanted to be **healthy** and **lean**.

This is the same friend who always says, "Man, you're in such great shape. How do you do it? What's your secret?"

There is no secret.

I had just shown him how.

I get the salmon and arugula instead of pasta.

I skip the ice cream.

If he started with those two changes, his life would improve **dramatically**.

There was obvious tension between us while he waited for his cup.

My friend felt that by not getting anything for myself, I was passing judgement on his choice to indulge.

But he was wrong.

I wasn't judging his **impulse** to get what he wanted.

He wanted ice cream.

I was following my **habit** of getting what I wanted.

I wanted to be able to take my shirt off when I was at the beach or a pool party and feel confident.

But that didn't change how he felt.

He felt weak, judged, and ashamed.

This triggered a cycle of self-talk everyone is much too familiar with:

> He felt judged.
>
> He resented me for judging him.
>
> He justified the choice to himself by insisting he deserved the ice cream because blah blah blah, fill in whatever bullshit excuse fits the situation.
>
> He found a way to convince himself it was about external factors, or me, instead of himself.

He said, "You're full of shit, man. I've seen your Instagram posts, like, 'Life is short. Eat ice cream.'"

"Oh, for sure," I said. "If it's your birthday or some other special occasion, or if I'm on vacation, I'll get ice cream with you. You'll be astounded by how much ice cream I can put away. I'll eat you under the ice cream table."

He looked confused.

"But today is Sunday," I said. "I just had an amazing dinner. I feel light and energetic. If I get that cup of ice cream, I might enjoy the hell out of it. But fifteen minutes from now I'll feel like garbage. Tomorrow I'll feel bloated. I don't want that. I **don't want that** more than I **do want the ice cream**."

He nodded.

He understood.

He ate the ice cream.

And we both got exactly what we **wanted**.

Willpower Won't Power You

After we left the ice cream shop my friend said, "Man, I wish I had your willpower."

I burst out laughing.

"Oh no you don't! I have zero willpower. My willpower sucks."

"Well, it's still stronger than mine. I got the ice cream and you didn't."

"That's not willpower. That's **habit**. The ice cream wasn't even a choice for me. I never considered it an option."

"So, what, one day you just said you weren't having ice cream anymore? Except on birthdays?"

"No way man. I just made tiny, incremental changes over a long period of time.

Did I ever tell you about how I quit smoking?"

"No."

So we found a spot to sit, and he ate his ice cream and I told him.

I used to smoke a pack to a pack and a half a day. This was after I became sober and was actually trying to be healthy. I know, it sounds stupid, and it was.

I was clinging to the habit of smoking because it got me through detox and rehab. I was still incredibly anxious and high-strung, and smoking helped me calm down and suppress my emotions.

Bottom line though, I was addicted to it and thought it looked cool. Most of the time.

But I was eating relatively clean, doing yoga, and exercising, and I started to gain an awareness about my body and overall health. I started to question what smoking was really doing to me.

What benefit am I getting from it?

Is it serving me?

What is the upside?

This took me back to a conversation I had with the beautiful Bob Forrest, who drove me to the Pasadena Recovery Center in 2003 after I'd gone blind and paralyzed in that ditch.

He told me to take a sheet of paper and make two columns, then write two lists. A list of benefits, and a list of consequences—pros and cons, basically—about my drug addiction.

As you can imagine, the columns were severely uneven.

So I did the same with my smoking habit and got similar results. The benefits were few and flimsy:

1. Calms me down. (But so did taking a sauna or going for a walk.)

2. Slows my breathing. (But so did yoga.)

3. Makes me look cool. (Um, no.)

The consequences filled the entire second column:

1. Increased chance of cancer.

2. Killing my teeth and gums.

3. Horrible breath.

4. Stench on my skin and clothes.

5. High blood pressure.

6. Makes me look like a jackass. (This one was hard to realize.)

On and on…

So I decided I was going to quit smoking.

But not in one day.

I'd tried going cold turkey before with drugs, alcohol, and smoking. It was miserable and never worked.

The only time it did work—when I finally got sober—was because I knew if I didn't stop doing heroin and cocaine immediately I was going to die.

Smoking didn't quite have that urgency, even though it was certainly chipping away at my lifespan. But I knew I needed to quit.

Even more important: I finally **wanted** to quit.

So I made a tiny, incremental change I knew was attainable.

I told myself and everyone around me I was only going to smoke ten cigarettes a day.

It was important for me to broadcast this fact to my friends, just like I did the day before I left Ohio. I told my friends I was leaving, going to California, and they said, "Bullshit. You've been saying that for years."

Having them call me out like that put tremendous pressure on me to follow through. My pride wouldn't let me fail. I knew I'd need that motivation to quit smoking, because willpower alone wasn't going to cut it.

So I told everyone my limit was ten a day, and I'd tell them what number I was on.

"This is number six."

"This is ten. Last one for the day."

Some of them thought I'd fail, or sneak away for number eleven, twelve, twenty... but I didn't.

I stuck with ten a day for a few months, then told everyone I was cutting down to five a day.

I did that for a few months, then I cut down to three a day.

When I got down to three a day, I thought, "This is so fucking stupid. Why am I still smoking at all?"

I also started a bunch of new habits at that time, like going to yoga more consistently, drinking green juice and shots of ginger, lemon juice, and apple cider vinegar, taking vitamins, etc. etc. etc. And by that point it was easy to quit altogether.

I had built a solid foundation of small changes, and by the time I quit, my habit of not smoking was stronger than my habit of smoking.

It was that simple.

But if I had tried to just up and quit on day one, I'd have failed. I'd have been back to smoking within twenty-four hours, guaranteed.

Using the power of tiny changes to establish new, sustainable habits, I gradually made a massive improvement to my overall health and happiness.

The Prison Pizza

"Okay," my friend said. "I can see that approach with smoking. I mean, that's a disgusting habit with zero benefits. But with food, it's different. I'm still getting nutritional value from a burger and fries."

"You're getting **calories**," I said. "That's not the same thing as nutrition. You're also clogging your arteries and creating massive amounts of inflammation in your body."

"But still, say I go from twice a week to once a week. Then once a month. I guarantee you I'm gonna spend the whole goddam month thinking about that burger. And I don't have the willpower to fight that."

"I guarantee you won't. Buddy, I guarantee that if you get it down to once a month, at some point you'll look around and realize you haven't had a burger and fries in three or four months. The newfound energy you'll feel, plus all the compliments you'll get, combined with your sense of accomplishment all start to outweigh the desire for junk food. On a deeper level, when you embark on a journey of self-care you begin to experience a whole new love. Self-love, loving yourself. It's habit, man. Not willpower. You want to know how weak my willpower is?"

Then I told him about the pizza.

I was meeting a friend at the original SunLife Organics in Point Dume, which happens to be very close to what I consider to be among the best pizza on the planet, D'amore's Pizza.

Now, I was all set to grab some salmon and steamed vegetables for dinner—my **habit**—when the pizza shop's owner Joe D'amore walked in.

As soon as I saw him my mouth started watering. I forgot about salmon and vegetables.

All I could think about was D'amore's Pizza…

Joe looked at me and smiled. He's probably seen the look millions of times.

He said, "You want a pizza?"

"Yeah."

It just tumbled out of my mouth instantly. So much for willpower, right?

Joe said, "Call Joe Junior, he's over there right now. Order whatever you want, my treat."

I picked up the phone like a man possessed and called D'amore's. Joe Junior must have recognized the incoming number, because he picked up and said, "Hey buddy, how are you?"

"I'm great, and I'm actually here with your dad. Can I order one of the individual gluten-free pizzas?"

I figured I could mitigate the damage a little by getting gluten-free, maybe even convince myself it wasn't really pizza.

Joe Senior said, "What are you talking about? Gluten-free, you don't need gluten-free. You don't have celiac. Get it the regular way."

And because my willpower is so strong, I said into the phone, "Well, I guess I'm not having the gluten-free."

When the pizza arrived it had six slices, plenty for two or three people. Unless one of those people is me, because I ate it all.

Joe D'amore, the genius and artist who has been making pizza for over thirty years, watched me stuff that one into my face. He burst out laughing.

"I have never in my life seen someone enjoy a pizza as much as this. Ever."

I was too busy hunching over the pizza with one arm wrapped around it to care.

"Look at you," Joe said. "It's like you're in a prison cafeteria, guarding that thing with your life."

I didn't speak until I was down to the final piece of crust, dipping it all into Ranch dressing.

"This is the best pizza I've ever had."

And all it took was Joe coming in and asking if I wanted one. I knocked my habit aside and tried to rely on my willpower to make a good decision for me, and that lasted exactly zero seconds.

In that moment, I **wanted** that pizza more than I **wanted** to stick to the habit I'd formed over years.

And you know what?

That's okay.

I knew I'd go right back into my habits the next day. I wouldn't even think about what to have for breakfast the following morning, because I don't eat breakfast, and that habit is so established.

I wouldn't rely on willpower.

And thankfully, Joe D'amore wasn't going to burst into my home at 5:30 in the morning and ask if I wanted a pizza for breakfast.

Because I'd say yes!

Doritos

Outside the ice cream shop, my friend didn't seem too impressed by what I considered to be a massive failure of willpower.

"I mean, it's D'amore's," he said. "Of course you're gonna say yes. Just like saying no to smoking is a no-brainer."

"Maybe," I said. "How do you feel about Doritos?"

"Doritos? Which kind?"

"Doesn't matter. Take your pick."

He shrugged. "They're okay."

"Just okay," I said. "Not amazing or anything?"

"Nah. Not like D'amore's pizza, if that's what you're getting at."

"Okay. Because if you showed up tonight with a bag of Doritos on you, even stashed away in a suitcase, I'd know."

He frowned. "What do you mean, you'd know?"

"I'd sense them. I'd smell them. I would just know there were Doritos nearby, and I'd find them and eat them."

And I would.

This goes back to when I was a neglected kid eating whatever I wanted—pizza and Doritos, basically—because no one was there to tell me otherwise. That stuff became my comfort food, my security blanket.

Even now I have an agreement with myself: When I'm sick, I treat myself to Doritos, pizza, and a glass bottle of Mexican Coke.

I know they're terrible for me and go against everything I should be doing to get back to one-hundred percent.

But in those moments, I **want** the comfort and happiness I get from a bag of Doritos, pizza, and Coke more than I **want** to be healthy. And strangely enough, nine times out of ten I actually get better. It's probably a placebo effect or the simple act of rebellious self-love. Regardless, eating Doritos, pizza, and Coke two or three times a year isn't going to kill me.

But eating it every day will.

So when I'm sick, the people close to me will bring over a bag of Doritos, pizza, and Coke and I'll devour it. Sometimes they try to be sneaky and stash an extra bag of Doritos in my house for later. Their intentions are good.

But then they quickly realize something:

There is no hiding Doritos from me.

I've had friends rip a bag out of my hands and throw them in the garbage.

"You're right," I say. "I shouldn't eat those."

And I wait.

I bide my time.

As soon as they leave, I dig that bag out of the trash and eat whatever is left.

Am I proud of this?

Not really.

But I'm not ashamed either.

I know myself.

I know that 99% of the time I can't have crap like that in my house.

If it's near me, I'll eat it.

The 1% of the time when I partake, I allow myself to enjoy it.

What's the point of indulging and feeling guilty?

Once you know yourself and your story, and control it fully, you can and should indulge.

Treat yourself and don't feel guilty about it.

But when that moment is over, throw the empty Doritos bag away and get back to your **habits**.

This theory DOES NOT apply to drugs and alcohol, infidelity, or anything else that can instantly kill you or destroy your life.

I didn't see the mud.

I didn't see the razor wire.

I saw the finish line (even though it was out of view and four miles away)!

Allow yourself to dream.

Visualize what you want.

See it and speak it as if it has already come to fruition.

Write down your goals.

Keep it simple and concise.

If you get knocked down get back up.

If you can't get back up then crawl—but do not stop until you cross the finish line.

Just One

If you want to eat better, start with one green juice or smoothie a day.

Just one.

If you want to exercise more, start with one ten-minute walk a day.

Just one.

Because if you go from zero exercise and eating shit all day to a full-blown vegan intermittent fasting diet with three CrossFit WODs a day, you're going to crash and burn in less than a week. Change that massive is not sustainable.

But I guarantee you:

If you start with **just one** change...

And that change becomes a **habit**…

And you add **just one** more change...

And **that** change becomes a habit…

You will gradually establish a change so massive it will seem like an evolution of you as a human being.

You won't recognize yourself.

You won't recognize your life.

And you'll love it.

Start with **just one**.

Unless...

Start with just one small change—**unless** you won't live long enough to make it into a habit.

Look, eating clean and exercising are vital for finding and fulfilling your true purpose in this life.

But if you're shooting heroin into your veins, smoking crack or meth, or drinking yourself into oblivion every night, one small change isn't going to cut it.

You don't have that luxury.

You don't have that kind of time.

Trust me, I was there.

Guess what would have happened if I had crawled out of that roadside ditch, temporarily blind and paralyzed, and said, "Hey, starting tomorrow I'll just snort a little less pure cocaine. And I'll toss in a kale smoothie."

I'd be dead.

I needed a massive, sweeping change just to keep me alive. But even that massive, sweeping change I did one day at a time. Any of us can do anything one day at a time. You need food to live, but can go an entire day without eating and be just fine.

If your child or loved one was in danger twenty miles away, you could walk and run all day to get there and help them. Trust me, you would not stop moving until you got there, even if it took all day. And the next. And the next.

But could you do the same to save yourself? Yes, if you attack it one day at a time.

Massive change can seem incredibly intimidating. But looking at it in twenty-four hour increments makes it much easier to digest. You get through one day, sleep like a baby, and wake up to a new one day. Your goal is not one year, one month, one week. Just one day. Break it down to one hour if you have to.

My abstinence from drugs and alcohol has only and ever been accomplished one day at a time. At this point, I've been doing it for 6,000 straight days.

6,000 days ago, I needed help.

If you're dealing with the same things I was, you need help too.

You need help to scrape yourself off of rock bottom and get back to zero.

Only then can you start making the tiny changes that will take you to soaring heights of abundance and happiness.

If that's where you are, here are some wonderful people and places who can help: khalilrafati.com/rehab.

This is It

This is the part in the book where you get hooked and you make the decision and you never look back.

This is the first moment and the first day of the rest of your life.

You will look back on this day fondly and you will smile and you will tell other people about this moment, when the big shift happened when change came to town!

You are going to look back in a couple years and you will be absolutely astonished at where you are, how you look, and how you feel!

In the end it's not going to be this book that is responsible for all of the magical and profound life-altering change that is going to take place.

You are going to be responsible.

You and you alone.

It was the moment I realized I am 100% responsible for everything going on in my life-both good and bad-that the massive, magical, monumental change began to take place.

DROP YOUR OLD STORY: RECOVER FROM WHATEVER IS HOLDING YOU BACK

"People fall so in love with their pain, they can't leave it behind. The same as the stories they tell. We trap ourselves."

— CHUCK PALAHNIUK

You Are the Author

If you want your story to be amazing, you must first start by realizing that you are the author and every day is a new page.

You can literally begin right now and completely change the trajectory of your life in such a profound way that within a short period of time you will barely recognize yourself in the mirror.

It does not take intelligence or strength or good upbringing.

It does not take higher education.

It does not require elite God-given talents.

It does not matter in any way how old you are or what your financial circumstances are.

It's not at all about putting in massive effort and going as hard and as fast as you can.

All it takes is making the shift. The shift from deluding yourself into believing that life is something that happens to you, into understanding that life is what you make it.

A tiny shift of small, seemingly insignificant actions that ultimately become habits.

A tiny shift away from distractions into actions.

This tiny shift is just like that tiny snowball we all hear about at the top of the mountain that starts to roll down and gains momentum and ultimately becomes an avalanche.

Or that single acorn that randomly gets buried in the ground by some over industrious, manic and forgetful squirrel. That tiny acorn grows into a giant tree with thousands of acorns appearing on it every spring, and over time that tiny acorn has turned into a massive forest.

A tiny, seemingly insignificant shift practiced on a daily basis over a sustained period of time creates an avalanche of success. A forest of abundance and prosperity. An amazing and incredible life so profound that you will be talked about for generations to come!

Is that too bold of a statement?

Listen, I was living under a bridge in my 30s, unable to make it through the day without shooting myself full of heroin and cocaine. There was no chance in hell that I was going to make it out of that situation, and yet here I am, 16 years later, healthier and happier than I've ever been.

I was literally unemployable my entire life and yet now I employ over 400 people!

Think about that for a moment.

Think about that and embrace this: If a fucking moron like me can crawl my way out of hell and live the life that I'm living, anybody can!

So, are people going to be talking about you for generations to come?

That is for you to decide.

Most people will never make this shift. Most people will spend their lives bloated and unhappy, shuffling their way towards failure and regret. Some might even seem successful on the surface.

But deep down inside are their unfulfilled dreams.

Deep down inside is the song of their soul, forever left unsung.

So they begin using alcohol, cigarettes, sex, pills, shopping, gambling, social media, marijuana, codependency, gossip, drama, religion, food, etc. etc. to numb themselves and mask their pain and avoid the unbearable truth that we only get one life and the amount of time that we have left is probably far less than we care to admit.

This shit goes fast. The older we get, the faster time flies by.

The unbearable truth that we are going to die and there is absolutely nothing we can do about it.

This truth is so unbearable that almost everyone will choose distractions, mediocrity and complacency.

Most people will choose comfort even if it is slowly strangling them to death.

Most people will desperately cling to what is familiar because the idea of change is so terrifying.

Most people will choose comfort regardless of the side effects and comfort makes cowards of us all.

The choice is yours.

WAKE UP!!!

Live your dreams.

Realize your purpose and destiny.

Live with passion!

Or stay asleep.

Stay the same.

Tell yourself again that someday you'll change but not until…

And go on living with an underlying level of fear and anxiety that will slowly eat away at your soul until there's nothing left.

Old, fat, deeply unhappy and full of regrets.

ARISE

AWAKE

ASCEND!!!

Freedom

Freedom from addiction/alcoholism.

Freedom from self-loathing/self-hatred.

Freedom from the dysfunction of my family and upbringing.

Freedom from epigenetic imprinting.

Freedom from poverty.

Freedom from cognitive dissonance

Freedom from codependency and dysfunctional relationships.

Freedom from the opinions of sad and broken people who cannot bear to see others happy.

Freedom is the ultimate high and ultimate goal! Life without freedom is slavery. Life without freedom has very little true happiness or meaning.

Our captors hide behind many veils. We all suffer from Stockholm Syndrome and spend our lives making excuses and defending the circumstances and situations keeping us hostage.

I had a long list of captors but I am eternally grateful to be free. I hope your list is much shorter!

What is keeping you hostage? What story are you telling yourself to justify it?

Let it go, surrender.

Drop your story and ask God for help and one day at a time, maybe one hour at a time, walk away and don't ever look back!

Create new habits, build new relationships. Know that you deserve to be happy and to be loved!

Fear will creep in even at the very notion of this. The ego will tell you, "Well, things aren't that bad..." or, "Okay, maybe I'll start tomorrow..."

There is no tomorrow.

I have a very brief amount of time left on this planet and my sincere, passionate goal is to inspire as many people as I can to live a life of freedom filled with happiness and meaning.

What You Focus on You Become

What you put your energy into, what you talk about, what you are angry about, what you are hopeful and happy about all becomes and manifests into your physical reality.

Our words, our thoughts, and our actions all become our physical realities and our day-to-day existence. If you're a geeky vegetarian dude obsessed with coding and hanging out in your garage with other people that are obsessed with coding and you constantly talk about and envision yourselves changing the world you will most likely change the world. Maybe even in a monumental way.

If you are a disenfranchised man frustrated with the world and your life and you hang out with other disenfranchised men full of anger that slowly turns to hatred, you may find yourself grabbing onto convictions. Your anger and hatred will grow as you put more thoughts and feelings and emotions into them and into those around you. Sooner or later with enough cognitive bias and encouragement you might come to believe that strapping a bomb to yourself is a great idea.

If you were taught to love money or even to greatly appreciate it when you were a child you will begin to accumulate money which, like everything else, is energy. You will strike up conversations with relatives or strangers and you will begin learning more and more about money and how to make it, to save it, and how not to lose it. Help comes from everywhere including the universe and chances are by the time you become an adult, even a young adult, you will have financial independence.

But let's flip that around.

If you grow up in a poor neighborhood with a single mother who is gone all day working and you witness all the poverty around you but you see certain men driving fancy cars and wearing beautiful flashy clothes and brand new Air Jordans, you will learn different lessons.

You will come to understand that violence and power are the only tools to lift you out of your despair and poverty. You will most likely begin committing crimes and violence against your brothers, against your neighbors or schoolmates. By the time you are a young adult you will most likely be incarcerated or dead.

Our external world influences our thoughts and our beliefs. The greatest advice ever given to me was by Rick Rubin. The first piece of advice he offered was that I needed to meditate. I didn't know him and he didn't explain himself, and when I questioned why he just repeated himself, "You need to meditate."

After getting to know him and having my life profoundly impacted by incorporating meditation, he gave me the second piece of greatest advice that I've ever heard. He told me to never watch the news. Again I frantically asked him why, over and over. He put his finger up and waved it back-and-forth and said never, ever, ever watch the news.

"Don't be satisfied with stories, how things have gone with others.

Unfold your own myth."

– RUMI

Convictions

Convictions are dangerous.

Do not become a convict of your own beliefs.

Up in Flames

> "I don't know what's gonna happen, but I wanna have my kicks before the whole shithouse goes up in flames."
> — JIM MORRISON

That is some bad, bad advice. Whether the "shithouse" is the world, your marriage, your job, or your body, that sort of fatalistic approach totally lets you off the hook and enables bad habits, behavior, and treatment of yourself and others.

Unfortunately, I latched onto it like a life preserver when I was a kid, and the "shithouse" was my life. It confirmed everything I'd been told by others and myself:

You're worthless.

You're a piece of shit.

You're not good enough.

What's the point of any of this?

Do whatever the hell you want.

Just go numb.

Nobody cares and you're going to die anyway.

"I don't know what's gonna happen, but I wanna have my kicks before the whole shithouse goes up in flames."

It was my anthem. All of a sudden my actions and attitudes were justified. Hell, even romanticized. I was sixteen, seventeen, eighteen and went looking for proof that the world was a terrible place and found it everywhere, because that's all I was trying to find. Pretty soon I was on an IV feed of punk rock, Charles Manson, Jim Jones, two liters of Pepsi, cheap pizza, and fuck you world along with whatever drugs I could get my hands on.

What a recipe for disaster.

When I moved to California, thinking that would make everything better, I dragged my old story with me like an anchor. It was my tinderbox, ready and waiting for the day when the whole shithouse went up in flames.

The whole time I was partying, buying and selling drugs, and living what I thought was an amazing life, I talked endlessly about having been sexually abused as a child. I kept reliving the past. I told anyone who would listen that I was dumb, ugly, destitute, and unlovable. I was still full of self-pity, jealousy, and rage, because that's what my story demanded. What else could I possibly feel after what I'd been through?

In 2003, days away from imminent death, I hit my threshold for pain. It simply became too much to bear. I did not have the will nor the strength to carry on. So I surrendered. I got sober.

Mercifully, I met a man named Robbie, who became my sponsor in a 12-step recovery program. Robbie bought me my first cellphone and a pair of decent shoes (I had hand-me-down boots that smelled like fermented cabbage). Robbie showed me that I was repeating the same sad story about my life and myself over and over and over again, ad nauseam.

Then one day Robbie asked me: "Who would you be if you dropped your old story?"

I was confused. "Drop my story? But that's who I am."

"No it's not. You're whoever you choose to be. Your story is up to you. You are the author of your life. Why not make it a great story instead of a tragedy?"

That question has never left me.

What if, as a young man, I had found classical music instead of flaming shithouses?

What if I had put clean, fresh, organic food into my body instead of processed gluten and dairy and high fructose corn syrup?

What if I hadn't worked so hard to anesthetize myself from the reality that my soul is on this plane of existence for evolution, not destruction? That I have a purpose, to fulfill my divine, intended potential, just like you do?

Would I be where I am today?

I think so. Because I am on the path of my potential, and whether I started down this path at fourteen or thirty-four doesn't matter. It saddens me to think about that lost child, neglected and abused and furious at the world, but I also have to smile when I look back on how things used to be, how I used to be, and how much everything has changed. How much I have changed that story.

With the help of my creator and some wonderful human beings I was able to change.

You might be in the shithouse right now. It might even be going up in flames as you read this, and you've been dancing in the fire, waiting for it to consume you and make all the pain go away.

I promise you that is not your story. I don't know what your true story is—only you and whatever creator you believe in do—but I do know you will find it through grace, time and change.

And through grace, time and change, you will look back at this flaming shithouse and smile.

"Artists are people driven by the tension between the desire to communicate and the desire to hide."

—DONALD WOODS WINNICOTT

My shithouse did go up in flames, eventually. It was a glorious bonfire of release and celebration and love when I finally let go of the story I was telling myself. I stopped living my life according to that tired script and started living my truth.

By the way, did I ever once consider how those words served the person who spoke them? Did I ever, in the stupidity and arrogance in my youth, ask, "What happened to the man who created that anthem?"

Here was this beautiful, young poet blessed with gorgeous looks, a perfect physique, and god-given talents who let the fame and fortune go to his head, and then fueled by drugs and alcohol wound up dying a bloated, drunken slob, alone in a bathtub, at the age of 27. What a great person to take advice from.

Don't get me wrong, I can still appreciate some of The Doors' music, but I don't want to be Jim Morrison. I want to be Mark Sisson. I want to be Joe Rogan. I want to be Rich Roll. I want to be Richard Branson, Tom Ford, Tony Robbins, etc. etc.

I know it's late in life, but I want to get married and have kids and be ripped and strong and travel and do awesome shit. I don't want to be a fat, bloated slob who dies alone in a bathtub.

Struggle = Strength

"Think training's hard? Try losing."

— TJ DILLASHAW, UFC

Believing Your Own Bullshit

In 2001 I lived on Heathercliff Road in Malibu with my girlfriend at that time. When she went to Europe for three weeks with her family, I forgot to pay the water bill because I was too busy shooting coke and heroin around the clock.

I was still shitting in the toilet even though there was no water to flush. There were swarms of flies in the bathroom. After two weeks I was so dehydrated from shooting up and not drinking any water I became constipated, which was sort of a relief because of the whole no water thing, but I was in agony because of the giant shit inside of me that desperately needed to come out.

I could stick my finger up my ass and feel it in there. I tried to pull it out, but it kept slipping back up into my colon. After seven days I got so desperate from the pain I took a pencil and stuck it up my ass to pry the feces out.

The pencil slipped and ruptured the inside of my anus and blood spurted everywhere. It covered my hands, the toilet, and the mountain of shit that had piled up over the weeks.

And yet I still somehow felt I was okay.

I didn't need to get sober or go to treatment.

My bathroom looked like a slaughterhouse, I had blood pouring out of my ass, and I hadn't shit in three days. The only thing I wanted was more coke and heroin.

Take a good, long look in the mirror. Hopefully you aren't sitting on a heaping pile of shit and blood with flies swarming around your face while you do it.

Ask: What bullshit story am I telling myself right now?

Sorry, I know that's a graphic story, but it's the truth.

Living in shit and squalor and blood, I was still able to convince myself that I was fine, everything was fine, that I didn't need to change.

Do you need to change? Are you deluding yourself, rationalizing, minimizing, and justifying your behaviors?

Please, please, please don't let things progress to the point I did.

Be honest with yourself and make the necessary changes now before your health or circumstances become as dire as they did for me, because sometimes things cannot be reversed.

I was told I was stupid my whole life. I was told that I would never amount to anything. My own father called me a bum and a prima donna whore. No matter what I did, I was never good enough in his eyes. My mother taught me poverty and how to maintain a poverty mentality. I spent most of my life not just in fear but in terror. I listened to them and I listened to those miserable teachers who belittled me and put me down and told me how bad I was all the time. I allowed the voice inside my head to resonate with their voices and I listened and I believed.

And then one day I woke the fuck up!

This is my life and I'm going to make it an amazing life and no one is going to stop me!

Fuck all of those naysayers. Fuck all of those broken people who tried to keep me down. All of them are crabs in a fucking basket. Gross little sea bugs crawling around and eating shit off of the seafloor.

I control the voice inside my head now. I control my reality and my destiny. I am powerful beyond measure!

I am God's son and he bestows his power and grace upon me and I graciously accept it!

Cognitive Dissonance

"People will do more to avoid pain than they will do to gain pleasure."

— TONY ROBBINS

Even though I was in tremendous pain from that constipation and dehydration, I knew it was nothing compared to the pain of withdrawal and detox. That's why I convinced myself I was fine. It matched my desire to avoid the greater pain.

And of course it was total bullshit. I was in much greater pain mentally, emotionally, and spiritually as an addict, but that didn't fit the story I told myself. It's an extreme case of cognitive dissonance, the state of mind that occurs when evidence clashes with belief.

Telling myself I was absolutely fine while perched atop a throne of shit and blood is a pretty blunt example. But one of the most insidious things about cognitive dissonance is that it can be extremely subtle while completely destroying your life.

Like when I was smoking. I knew it was terrible for me and there is enough evidence out there to carpet the moon, but I believed it made me look cool and it wasn't really doing that much damage. The comfort I got from smoking was greater than the comfort I would get from being healthier.

It's a slightly less harsh example of cognitive dissonance, but still pretty overt when you consider the physical act of smoking, the odors, the mess.

How about exercise? Always healthy and more is better, right? Tell that to the triathlete who can't walk because they ran the cartilage out of their joints, ignoring the pain because they believed they needed to push through it. The pain of swimming and biking and running was more comfortable than the pain of stopping.

Or my dumb ass, again. (It's always easy to find terrible examples for this book, because I lived so many of them.) I love yoga. It heals me, helps me check in with my body and breath to see where I'm holding tension, anger, and trauma.

The evidence is clear. When I do yoga, I'm more centered, happier, and just a better all-around person.

But as an addict, I convince myself the surge of serotonin, dopamine, and testosterone I get from lifting heavy weights is just as beneficial. I also like the way it makes me look and the compliments that follow, and it's easy to convince myself that is just as important as my inner state.

I have abs—absolutely nothing.

The Only Thing that Stops Me

And if I tried, maybe I could convince myself it's too much of a hassle to get to the yoga studio, it's too expensive, I don't like the instructors...but no. Because here's the thing: I live next door to the yoga studio that I own!

And I still manage to believe I shouldn't do yoga more often.

Why? If I'm comfort seeking, isn't yoga more comfortable than the all-out effort of lifting heavy weights?

No! Not for me, anyway. Lifting heavy weights makes me stronger. Tougher. It's explosive and makes me feel like an athlete. It makes me look like a fighter, and if I'm a fighter I can beat the hell out of anything that tries to hurt me, or at least look like I can.

Yoga is about opening up. It's about letting go and being vulnerable. Lifting heavy weights is about making your outside look great. Yoga is the opposite. It's all about looking inward.

For me, being vulnerable is extremely uncomfortable. Which is exactly why I need to do it more often. It is lazy comfort seeking to do otherwise.

The only thing stopping me is me.

"He who looks outside dreams; he who looks inside awakens."

—JUNG

Do you think you're old? Go tell an 80-year-old how old you are. That you feel old. They will laugh in your face! Age is a number and an attitude. I have met 35-year-olds that bore the shit out of me and are unbearable to be around. So immature and full of themselves with their heels dug down deep into their convictions. How sad. And this is not unusual because most people die on the inside somewhere around 30. Unfortunately for them, and for the rest of us, they stick around another 40 to 60 years and become a burden on those who love them and society as a whole.

17 years ago when, by the grace of God, I began to turn my life around I was very fortunate to become friends with a man in his mid- to late-60s. He had mastered his craft and become incredibly wealthy, married a beautiful woman who loved him unconditionally, and was really truly on top of the world. He explained to me his great many troubles and all of the trials and tribulations associated with pursuing his chosen career. He floundered around for decades. And he too decided at a certain point to get his life together.

I'm not going to go into details because I don't have his permission to tell his story, but I will tell you he had no success until he was 54 years old. And when his success came, well you know the saying: When it rains it pours. And his success continues to pour like a monsoon!

His story had a huge impact on me. It changed my outlook on life, and my actual life.

I'm 49 years old as I write this. I'll be 50 in a month, and I can tell you that the 50-year-old version of me would kick the living shit out of the 25-year-old version of me. I am in the greatest shape of my life and I have never been happier, and that is saying a lot because I have done a lot of living.

Yes, of course I still battle my demons.

Yes, of course I still struggle from time to time with depression and anxiety, sometimes to a crippling degree.

But that is all part of my journey. A journey that never would have happened if I hadn't made the necessary changes and been inspired by people like my friend, who didn't find his version of success until he was almost 60.

When I first got clean and sober I could have thrown in the towel and settled for a life of mediocrity. But I inherently knew that if I didn't have an absolutely amazing life, sooner or later I would go back to the drink and the drugs.

I don't care if you're 20, 30, 40, 60, or 70.

The time to start walking toward your dreams is now.

Dissonant Love

The evidence is clear: Shooting coke and heroin and trying to perform a pencil enema is bad for you.

Smoking is bad for you.

Too much exercise is bad for you.

Seeking comfort at the expense of doing what you need to do is bad for you.

And the sneakiest forms of cognitive dissonance, the ones I believe cause the most people the most harm, are the toxic relationships we have with ourselves and others.

I was at a dinner with a group of friends, some I'd just met that night, and I overheard a young man at the table talking to the guy sitting next to me. They were talking about the young guy's girlfriend.

I heard him say, "No, I'm not. I'm not happy."

My neighbor said, "What would you need to do to be happy?"

A great question.

He answered, "Well, she would definitely have to stop drinking."

When he said it his voice got louder, and I don't think it was intentional. He didn't realize he was almost shouting. Of course, my ears perked up regardless of volume. Whenever someone starts talking about addiction I tend to lean in to see if I can help.

He said, "I mean, I love her. She's great. But she's got to get her shit together. I had to pay her rent a couple of times. It's just a mess. I want to move back out here, but I don't want to move in with her."

Then the guy next to me started talking about his relationship and how amazing it is. How much he loves his girlfriend and how all they want to do is spend time together. It wasn't to rub the other guy's nose in it—he was trying to let him know that relationships don't need to have that kind of toxicity. They shouldn't, in fact.

The way he talked sounded exactly how I feel about my girlfriend. I was lucky enough to get invited on this crazy vacation in the south of France. We were spending time on mega yachts, helicopters, and moving back and forth between Paris, Cannes, San Tropez, and Antebbe. It was visually stunning and the food was amazing, but all I wanted to do was get back home so I could snuggle up with her and watch Netflix. We're so comfortable together there is literally nowhere else in the world we'd rather be than with each other.

The guy with the toxic relationship wanted whatever comfort it brought him more than he wanted the pain of ending it. Maybe he was terrified of being alone. Maybe he got fulfillment out of her needing him to take care of her. Whatever it was, he believed he was comfortable when all of the evidence—most of it coming straight out of his mouth—showed he was actually miserable.

He said, "I don't know what to do."

I couldn't stay quiet any longer.

I said, "What do you mean you don't know what to do?"

He looked at me. "I just don't, man."

"Of course you know what you do. You need to break up with this girl. You are enabling her. If you really love her and care about her like you say you do, do you think you're helping her by paying her rent and allowing her to flounder and continue drinking herself blind?"

He was shocked. Not like, "How dare you talk to me like that?" shocked.

He was shocked because someone had actually given voice to the truth he already knew. His cognitive dissonance was being shattered.

I said, "Look man, I'm sorry, I don't have a filter. I'm just telling you the truth. And you know this is the truth. I'm not telling you anything you don't know."

He stared at me for a few seconds, then said, "You're right."

The person he supposedly loved, and who supposedly loved him, was ruining his life. He was helping her do it. And he was probably helping her ruin her life by enabling her.

He wanted to move back to California but dreaded doing so because he'd have to move in with her.

He knew all of this. The evidence was obvious.

But he believed it was love and they needed to stay together. This fit the story he told himself, the one that kept him comfortable even though it was making him miserable.

What are you putting yourself through because you're too fearful to change?

What beliefs are you clinging to despite the mounting evidence to the contrary?

What is making you comfortable while it slowly kills you?

Notice: I did not ask **Who** is making you comfortable.

This isn't about them.

This is about your **relationship** with them.

You can't change someone else.

You can only change yourself.

You can only change your relationship with them.

Maybe that means a conscious uncoupling that makes you better friends than you ever were lovers.

Maybe that means clear, solid boundaries about what you will and won't accept going forward.

And maybe that change means ending the relationship completely.

And that's okay.

What is Your Why?

In his book *Start With Why*, Simon Sinek explains beautifully why having a purpose is so important—if you haven't read that book, do so.

Most people don't have a *Why*, or they've forgotten it along the way. It's painful to see these people walking around without an inner compass or a true understanding of who they are and what their purpose is.

Even more concerning are those who know their *Why* and have compromised it for short-term gain or success. I'm sure they didn't want that to happen. It probably started small, breaking a personal rule or value "just this once," but the moment we start compromising, it never ends.

It's so easy and comfortable to rationalize and justify these small choices. None of them feel like a life-changing decision. The marginal costs seem totally insignificant. But each tiny act, every small decision, these compound and eventually turn you into someone you never wanted to be.

Look at the people around you as you're shopping, walking, driving. Do most of them look happy and full of purpose? If they do, I want to know where you live.

When you're done looking around, look in the mirror. I mean literally stare into a mirror. Are you glowing with purpose and a life fulfilled? Or have you compromised those for something you thought was worth it?

The vast majority of us will secretly live a life of quiet desperation. We will spend our entire existence with the hidden, gnawing understanding that we are completely full of shit and completely lost.

We know deep down that we just walk around wearing different masks all day to try and please those around us. We leave our dreams unfulfilled. At our core we are terrified to try, to fail...we are terrified of being uncomfortable.

We choose comfort every time.

We anesthetize ourselves with small distractions: food, weed, booze/drugs, pornography, Facebook, Instagram, Pinterest, drama, gossip, work, etc. etc. etc.

We have become incredibly good at being busy. Busy being busy. Always busy. Like it's some badge of honor to be constantly harried. But it's a farce. It's just a coping mechanism to avoid the terrifying prospect of actually looking inward.

Then we see someone who is actually alive. Living with purpose, embracing their *Why*. Someone who got sick and tired of being sick and tired.

Someone who bottomed out and made the life-changing bold decision to end the cycle.

To wake up.

To become Awakened.

You recognize this immediately, even if you can't identify it.

They know their *Why*, and they do not compromise it for anything.

Feeding the Wolf

There is a famous allegory about the two wolves. An elder American Indian is teaching his grandson about life.

"A fight is going on inside me," he said to the boy. "It is a terrible fight and it is between two wolves. One is evil—he is anger, envy, sorrow, regret, greed, arrogance, self-pity, guilt, resentment, inferiority, lies, false pride, superiority, and ego."

He continued, "The other is good—he is joy, peace, love, hope, serenity, humility, kindness, benevolence, empathy, generosity, truth, compassion, and faith. The same fight is going on inside you. And inside every other person, too."

The grandson thought about it for a moment, then asked his grandfather, "Which wolf will win?"

The grandfather replied, "The one you feed."

I always return to the woods, to the mountains.

The birds here are crazy green wild parrots screeching and howling as they fly overhead or mock me from the trees up above.

The story goes that some super wealthy guy had this huge house here in Malibu and somehow all of his pet parrots got out one day and took off to live life on their own without cages, without confinement, without somebody else dictating the terms of how they would live their lives.

They are definitely not an indigenous species so I believe the story to be true and whether it is or not, every time I see or hear them I get a big smile on my face because there ain't nothing cooler than rebels, and these birds are some loud-ass vibrant green rebels!

There is something sacred about this canyon. I've heard all kinds of stories about Michael Landon and crazy Dr. Wagner, a.k.a. The Wizard, racing through here in the middle of the night naked on top of their horses, howling at the moon like madmen.

There are lots of snakes. Giant rattlesnakes, usually laying right in the middle of the path sunning themselves. I used to be scared of them until I looked up the symbolism of a snake. I'm no longer scared. I've seen bobcats on several occasions and I've even heard a mountain lion tracking me in the brush. And yes, that scared the shit out of me and I ran like hell.

There's a beautiful big tree where I will stop and sit and meditate from time to time. One time when I was having this crazy super deep meditation I had a strange compulsion to open my eyes and sitting in front of me, less than a few feet away, was a giant very well-fed coyote. We stared at one another for what seemed like an eternity. After our little staring contest was over she seemed to smile at me and nod her head, then turned and slowly trotted away and disappeared into the brush.

There are horses too. Lots of horses. About half the people who live in the nearby neighborhoods use this canyon to ride. On a hot day like today they are sweating just like me and their sweat gets everywhere, all over the brush. As I make my way through the canyon my body rubs against that same brush and their sweat and my sweat mixes together, creating a pungent scent. I love the smell.

I love the sun on my skin.

I love the smell of horseshit and sage and fennel all mixed in with my own smell.

I am an animal!

Fuck computers.

Fuck cell phones.

Fuck social media and society and all of its rules.

I am part angel, part beast!

It is very important that I make the best effort I can to be more angel than beast, but make no mistake about it—I am part beast.

I am wild and under the right circumstances could become quite savage. Society wants me to forget about my animal nature.

Fuck society!

Denying who you are or what you want will always end badly.

Love and embrace who you are and what you are.

Accept, acknowledge, embrace, and love it.

Then, and only then, can you begin to alter your thoughts and behaviors so you can be the best version of what you are.

Hawaii Journal

Up at 4 a.m.

Watched the sunrise.

Swam with sea turtles.

Ate gluten-free Mochi pancakes for breakfast topped with coconut and macadamia nuts.

So grateful to be alive and sober!

Grateful for the gift of desperation because nothing else would have allowed me to change.

It makes me shudder to think I almost missed all of this because I was so stubborn and clung so desperately to drinking and getting high and what I thought was right.

It's human nature to hang on to our ideas, stories, thought patterns, and habits. But what if they are no longer serving us or those around us?

What if they are robbing us of the ability to live a life beyond our wildest dreams?

What are you holding onto and unwilling to let go of that is no longer serving you?

"The unexamined life is not worth living."

—SOCRATES

Let Go of Your Fears

I lived most of my life in fear.

From an early age I was full of fear, anxiety and depression. Violence was constant in my early childhood, as well as neglect and sexual abuse and suicidal ideation. Most of that morphed into anger, resentment or jealousy of others as I got older.

Alcohol and drugs were a great coping mechanism to stave off the suicidal ideation, and in their absence the anger and resentment only grew. I wish I could tell you that when I got sober at 33 years old I snapped my fingers and it all disappeared. Unfortunately that is not the case.

It took many years of uninterrupted sobriety coupled with 12-step programs and constant introspection. Don't get me wrong—there were lots of good times in my early sobriety. Lots of small victories and tons of laughter. Much-needed deep and healing belly laughter. My friend Greg Solomon graciously fed me every day and kept me laughing. Sherman and Cindy Landon took me in like a stray dog.

And of course Robbie, my original sponsor, who thank God didn't understand that sponsoring somebody did not mean adopting them because he pretty much did just that for me. All these amazing people took such good care of me but I was still terrified. Without the drugs and alcohol the fear came back tenfold.

Ironically, I am immensely grateful for those hard times and my lack of resources. I bottomed out so hard that I became teachable. Being so destitute and dependent on others, I was also able to scrape together a tiny bit of much-needed humility.

As I write this, I am sixteen years sober and approaching my fiftieth year of life. I have fought and eliminated many fears. But one that has persisted—maybe because it makes me feel so powerless, so small, so insignificant—is my fear of water. The idea of getting pounded again and again by waves as I struggle toward shore makes me sick to my stomach.

And yet, I will face this fear too. I'm learning how to surf, because I am greater and stronger than my fear.

I will take it with me into the water and release it, set it free, and I will celebrate with the waves that used to terrify me.

Please, let go of your fears.

AUTHENTICITY

David vs. Goliath

One of the clearest examples of someone being authentic to their true self happened while I was on vacation in Hawaii. I was at a Bellator event with some great friends who happened to know Royce Gracie.

If you don't know who that is, let's pause for a few days so you can read up on how much of a legend this man is.

All caught up?

Just in case, Royce is the closest thing we've seen to a modern-day David from the David vs. Goliath parable. He and his family created the Ultimate Fighting Competition in 1993, then he won the entire tournament in UFC 1, 2, and 4 using Gracie Jiu Jitsu, which at the time was so mysterious it seemed like magic.

Royce was smaller, lighter, and almost always physically weaker than his opponents, yet he took every one of them down and either made them submit, choked them out, or broke a bone to win the fight.

He didn't showboat. He didn't have some grand entrance. In fact, he and about fifteen family members would all come in together like an anaconda, each man walking with his hands on the shoulders of the cousin, brother, father, or grandfather in front of him. This was—and is—a family of warriors, and I grew up idolizing what

Royce and the Gracies did inside the cage and ring.

I got into a lot of fights as a kid. I was always smaller. Almost always weaker. The underdog. But I never stopped fighting, just like Royce Gracie.

Now, that's as far as the comparison should go, if that. Royce is a legend and a champion. I was a punk kid who picked at least half the fights I got into, if not more, but in every one of those moments I felt threatened. It was hit or be hit, and I almost always hit first.

I didn't mention any of this to Royce, of course. I was thrilled and honored just to sit next to him at a Bellator fight. Simply sharing some time was enough for me, then Royce freaking Gracie turned to me and started talking about, get this, food and nutrition!

After a few minutes of sharing favorite organic foods and recipes, supplements, and which fruits go best together, it hit me that Royce had no idea who I was or what I did for a living. He was just chatting about stuff he liked to chat about.

Then things got very interesting. Someone handed Royce a box with a bottle of champagne in it.

My friend Kelly started laughing. He nudged me and said, "Watch this."

He pulled out his phone and tried to take a picture of Royce holding the champagne box, but Royce kept putting his arm over the label so its contents would be a mystery.

"Come on, move your arm," Kelly said.

Royce shook his head. "No, no, no, no."

They went back and forth, both of them laughing, and I turned to Royce's son and asked, "What's going on? Why doesn't he want Kelly to take the picture?"

"Oh, my family is very against alcohol. We think it is extremely destructive. We never put alcohol in our bodies. Never. Never."

I was speechless.

Again, they had no idea who I was, what I did, or what I'd gone through to get to this point in my life.

As an addict and alcoholic, as an abused and neglected child, the idea of an entire family dedicated to a clean lifestyle was beautiful. They wouldn't even be photographed with alcohol, let alone drink it.

And the thought of a family with a foundation of love and respect so strong that those values were passed from parent to child, and embraced by those children, nearly brought me to tears.

But talk about **authentic**...

Royce Gracie could have made millions of dollars endorsing one alcohol or another. He didn't have to drink it. He wouldn't even have to tell anyone he didn't drink it.

He could have just cashed the check and used it to buy enough organic fruits and vegetables to fill a stadium.

Instead, he stayed true to himself, his family, and his values.

He eventually put the champagne box down and we resumed chatting about juices and smoothies. Some might say a tad bit boring compared to the fights we were watching, or the epic battles Royce had been a part of.

I couldn't have been happier.

And I respected Royce Gracie more than ever.

There is only love. I know that's not a very profound way of saying that. If I cared to look smarter I could plagiarize some of the greats but that would be silly, there is only love.

I got out of a long-term committed relationship over two years ago and for the first time in my life at 46 years old I was single, sober, and successful which is a very powerful combination. I had been single many, many times in my youth, even desperately so. I was abstinent from drugs and alcohol at times during my youth but never long-term, and never sober-minded or sober in the sense of body and soul.

I also had brief moments of success, mostly in an egoic way and again, never long-term. So being single, sober, and successful all at the same time was an entirely new and exciting experience for me. Money and success opens quite a few doors that one could never imagine without experiencing it.

I purposely and intentionally played out every passion and desire and even every fantasy. I got into the best shape of my life, bought a fancy watch and a fancy car—in fact I bought several. Got myself a fancy haircut, some fancy cologne and some very fancy sunglasses that were so expensive I'm embarrassed to even think about it. My book and my business both became very successful at the same time and all of a sudden I was featured in the *New York Times* on the front page of Sunday's fashion and style section. CBS's morning show did a segment on me, as did ABC's Nightline. Even the BBC picked up my story and wrote about me. It was the craziest and strangest and most bizarre experience of my life!

Believe it or not, *Town and Country* magazine actually listed me as one of the top 50 most eligible bachelors in the world. LOL! I was on the same page as the guy who started Tesla and the guy who started Twitter. I literally could not believe my eyes when I saw it! I don't know how the hell it happened—they obviously ran out of cool people and somehow chose me.

All of a sudden I was getting direct messages on Instagram from some of the most ridiculously beautiful women I had ever seen, saying we should hang out. My response was always the same: "Why?!"

A month earlier, prior to all of this press and exposure, I was invisible to all of these women. I could've set myself on fire with gasoline in the middle of the street right in front of them and they most likely wouldn't have stopped to empty out one of their expensive water bottles to help extinguish the flames that were burning me alive!

The Heart-to-Heart Hug

I don't think hugs are supposed to hurt.

I see it all the time, and I'm guilty of it too. I walk up to a friend—usually it's another guy, because most of us are so awkward with affection—and we both have our chests puffed out to show how tough we are.

I lean way to my left, he leans way to his left, and we clamp our arms around each other with our butts sticking out. We slam each other on the back a few times then break apart before the insecurities run rampant.

My buddy Garrett McNamara showed me another way. I'll never forget the first time I tried to give him a grab-and-slap hug. We were in Hawaii, where Garrett lives, and I was shocked when he reached out and rested his hands on my shoulders to stop me.

He looked me in the eye and said, "No. That's shit-to-shit. This is heart-to-heart."

Then he leaned me to my right, put my left arm over his right shoulder and my right arm around his left side. He did the same with his arms, then stepped close and our sternums touched.

I could literally feel his heart beating, and he could feel mine. The shared energy was incredibly powerful.

After a couple seconds he stepped back and looked me in the eye again. No slaps, no pats, no karate chops. If either one of us had done that, the energy would have been broken.

"That's heart-to-heart," he said.

The way I'd been hugging, what Garrett called "shit-to-shit," puts your intestines up against the other person's intestines. Vital organs, for sure, but not great for sharing energy of love and connection.

I still forget sometimes and revert to the grab-and-slap, shit-to-shit hug. Sometimes I go for the heart-to-heart and the other person is going for shit-to-shit, so we're both leaning the same way and heading for a full-blown lip smack, which gets even more awkward.

Let's help each other out, just like Garrett helped me that first time. (And quite a few times since then…)

When you hug someone:

> Look them in the eye as you come together.
>
> Lean slightly to your right with your arms out.
>
> Put your left arm over their right shoulder.

Put your right arm around their left side.

Step into it. Don't lean in with your butt sticking out.

Wrap your arms around them and hold them close.

Press your heart to their heart.

Feel the energy. Share the energy.

After a few seconds, open your arms and step back.

Look them in the eye again.

Please do not slap or pat them. Doing so disrupts the flow of loving energy. This is especially common with males--I think it stems from nervousness or homophobia. Just embrace, heart-to-heart, and feel the love and energy between yourself and the other person.

And if you're a guy, and the other guy looks like Kelly Slater or Brad Pitt, hang on an extra few moments, ha ha ha!

That's the heart-to-heart hug.

I just wander around and think of you.

I have never in my life felt such love for another human being.

I miss your laughter.

I miss our silence.

I miss the funny looks you give me.

I miss buying you things.

I have been on billionaires' boats and eaten the fanciest meals in this luxury hotel, but nothing compares to eating a Chinese chicken salad with you and watching Netflix.

I am madly in love with you.

Please show this text message to your mother.

ADDICTION & RECOVERY

Why I Got High

I got high because it felt good. Because I was selfish. And ultimately, by the time I was smoking crack and heroin, I had stopped caring about other people.

I didn't care if me getting high hurt my girlfriend or my mother or my friends or anybody else. I did not care.

Yes, one of the reasons I **started** getting high was the trauma and neglect I experienced in my childhood. I was trying to fill a huge hole and I wanted to feel something other than despair. But once I got into the heavy stuff my addiction had nothing to do with my dad who beat me, or my mom who neglected me, or my step-brother who molested me. It was not their fault.

And I absolutely had a physical dependence on the drugs, but I don't blame that either.

I liked getting high. It felt good.

That's the bottom line.

People ask me all the time how they can save their child, their parent, their sibling, their friend from addiction. They care so much, and all they want to do is help. They're terrified about losing this person to addiction.

That's why it can be tough to tell them the truth, but they deserve to hear it.

"You can't save them. Kick them out. Cut them off. Cancel the cards and repossess the car. Do whatever you have to do to stop enabling them. That's the only way you can help."

Some people feel relieved when I tell them this. Like they finally have permission to do what they already know is necessary. But the fear and guilt at the thought of doing that to someone they love can be overwhelming.

They ask me, "But what if I cut them off and they die?"

My answer to that is just as blunt as my first response. "What if you keep doing what you're doing and they die?"

Because I've seen that happen. The enabling never stops and the addict dies, and the enablers feel responsible. They spend the rest of their lives asking, "What if..."

But I've seen hundreds of addicts, myself included, finally get help and get clean once the enabling stopped. The people who truly loved and cared cut them off to save them. The enablers were forced to show their heart by turning their back.

An addict has to want to change before anyone can help them.

Even then, it doesn't fall on loved ones to do the helping. If all you want to do is take the pain away from the addict, you can't help them. You're too close. Too invested in making them feel loved and comfortable.

Get them into a recovery program like Alcoholics Anonymous or Narcotics Anonymous where they can get the professional, firm, and compassionate help they need. What they do once they are in the program is up to them.

Am I an Addict?

Addiction is an equal-opportunity demon. It can be drugs, alcohol, sugar, video games, pornography, social media, exercise, shopping, surgery, politics—anything that drives you through rewarding stimuli to engage in compulsive behavior despite negative consequences.

Here's a scenario. You're walking down the street, scrolling through social media and pause long enough to wrinkle your nose at the heroin addict slumped in a doorway. Then you see some influencer's post about the new shoes they're repping and you immediately go to their profile and click the link.

You buy the same shoes using PayPal which runs through your credit card with 20% interest, a card which already has a balance you can't pay off, and post a photo of yourself in a casual, not-trying-to-be-cool pose.

For the next eight hours you refresh your feed to bask in the likes and comments. They make you feel all warm and fuzzy.

I have some bad news for you.

That bliss you felt when you bought the shoes?

The warm and fuzzies you got from the social media love?

The chemicals that made you feel that way are exactly the same as the heroin addict's rush.

Your compulsive need to get that social proof—post, refresh, repeat—is the same as some junkie cooking, tying off, and shooting up.

It's just cleaner and legal. But I would contend, equally if not more insidious.

Who Does This Serve?

For everything you do, every activity, every habit, every choice, ask yourself:

Is this serving me and those around me?

Is it bringing value to me and those around me?

The only thing we truly have, and can't get more of, is time—is this sucking your time away and wasting it?

If it isn't serving you and those around you, and it's wasting your time, stop for one day.

Is it easy? Or is it all you can think about?

Stop for one week.

Do you feel better or worse? Is your life better or worse?

Stop for one month.

Are you and those around you better served because you stopped?

If so, stop forever. Get help if you need to.

We don't have much time here. Stop wasting it by serving an addiction instead of yourself and those you care about.

Love is all there is.

If you found it, congratulations. You won life!

All the shiny materialistic shit feels good for a few days, maybe a few months...but love is all there is.

The love you have in friendship, in relationships, in family, in vocation...it's all that matters.

There's a janitor in Cleveland who's happier than any of us will ever be. Why? Because he loves his wife and kids, he loves his job and he loves the people in his community.

He feels like an asset and finds purpose and meaning in everything he does.

Love is all there is.

So-called "social media" will teach you the opposite.

Which is ironic, considering their economy of Likes and heart emojis...

Social media will teach you you're not good enough.

That being rich, or skinny, or famous, is all that matters.

It's all bullshit.

Love is all there is.

We are supposed to have belly fat-it's there to protect our organs.

It's natural.

We are supposed to have stretch marks because the body fluctuates in weight depending on the season, or our stress levels, or whether we're creating a baby.

We're supposed to have wrinkles-aging is natural and part of life.

If you think your political view is right and others are wrong, go home and hug your children.

If you think the dietary restrictions you placed upon yourself are going to save the planet, go volunteer at a soup kitchen or nursing home.

If you want to be an influencer, smash your smart phone with a hammer and go get a job, learn a skill, or create something that brings value into peoples' lives.

If you want to change the world, learn to love yourself.

And then love your neighbor as you would love yourself.

Start there and keep going.

Serving Love

If you're sitting at a table and they stop serving love, get up and walk away!

Twelve Steps

Twelve-step programs are amazing at helping with all sorts of problems: alcohol, drugs, debt, eating disorders, hoarding, sex, shopping—if you have an addiction or compulsion, chances are good there is a twelve-step group for it.

The meetings are full of people who care, know where you've been and what you're going through, and want to help. The time with those people, surrounded by their love and support, even when it's brutally honest, can be very comforting and encouraging. And that's great.

If you're going through that now or know you need to, do me a favor. First, make sure it's a free twelve-step program. Anyone who wants to take your money for this sort of group is a thief.

Then get in there, take the cotton out of your ears, stick it in your mouth, and be teachable.

Do exactly what they say. Every single day, pray for the willingness to have the humility to learn a different way of life. Get a sponsor.

I promise you, if you follow the steps you will change your life. And not just for kicking the addiction or behavior you're trying to shed. Applying those principles to self-care, relationships, and business will create amazing results. They will help you succeed at life.

But there is a catch. (Isn't there always?) It can be incredibly tempting and reassuring to dwell in those meeting rooms commiserating with others about how terrible life is, how everything is screwed up, how damaged we all are.

Do not live in those meeting rooms—make those rooms live in you.

You can't sit in meetings every day, maybe twice a day for the rest of your life and wonder why you're not happy or doing awesome shit.

I've seen hundreds of people stop drinking and using drugs just to get addicted to twelve-step meetings. Twelve-step programs are supposed to be bridges for us to get back into life. You don't go to high school forever. You don't go to college forever. You spend the time you need and you move along. I'm not suggesting you stop going altogether. I'm just warning you: Don't get addicted to twelve-step programs.

Once you're through the steps and come out the other side, get out and live your new happy, healthy, productive life. Implement the lessons you learned and enjoy the massive change you experienced.

Do your morning gratitude. Continue down your spiritual path. Take personal inventory of your life.

Just make sure you're doing it while you're out in the world living. There's nothing wrong with using twelve-step programs socially and lots of people find and hold a great sense of community in doing so, but there's a fine line between going socially and having it consume your entire existence.

This is a response to a just-sober young man bugging me for a job, or to hook him up with some rich people to employ him, or to make connections for him that will make his life and journey as a writer easier—basically asking me to clear away any obstacles and save him from putting in the labor.

"First, get a job and stop trying to figure out life. Get a disposable job, get a job at a coffee shop or yoga studio. Relax and take a deep breath. Go to meetings every day. Cut yourself a lot of slack and develop an attitude of gratitude. Begin meditating every morning without fail and by meditation I mean sit quietly for 10 minutes and focus on your breath. Stop trying to establish a career and identity when you're newly sober. Develop a network of sober friends and start to live a healthy lifestyle.

That should be your only focus, staying sober and being healthy physically, mentally, and emotionally. And stop asking me to give you a job, get you a job, or connect you with people who will do so. You are not helpless and you are more than capable of creating the type of life that you dream of living, but no one is going to hand that to you or connect you to it. You must do this on your own.

Sobriety has nothing to do with drinking/drugging. That's called abstinence. Sobriety is about growing up and taking full responsibility for yourself and your life. My job is to inspire you, not 'hook you up' or employ you or find you employment.

Focus on your sobriety and everything else will fall into place. Stop trying to make big decisions. You are in the infancy of sobriety. You are not even a caterpillar yet, let alone the beautiful butterfly that you can and hopefully will become. You are just a larva and hopefully you will stay sober long enough to become a caterpillar.

It is then and only then will you be graced with the opportunity to form your own chrysalis and take your journey inward to ultimately reemerge as the glorious butterfly.

Writers don't write because they want to, the same way painters don't paint because they want to. Writers write because they have to. Painters paint because they have to. Most of them are miserable and many spend way too much time engulfed in loneliness. Be careful what you wish for.

Go get a job. Take a deep breath. It's all gonna be okay if you allow it to be okay. Or keep struggling and trying to figure shit out. Up to you."

P.S.: I never heard from the guy again.

How and Why I Stayed Sober

In order to get sober I had to forget everything I thought I knew. Everything about who I was, what I was, and what I was supposed to do. I had to forget what I thought would make me happy.

Every morning, I'd wake up and repeat: "I don't know anything. The voice inside my head will harm me if I pay attention to it. The voice inside my head is not my spiritual advisor no matter how many times it tries to convince me otherwise. My ego is not my amigo. I don't know anything..."

It was basically taking the story of myself and my life and deleting all of it, leaving only a blank page. Which was good, because I'd made a complete mess of my life. My mind was broken, my thoughts were destructive, and I knew if I could just shut up, listen, and learn, I just might survive.

I went to meetings every day, seven days a week, sometimes multiple times a day. I ran through the steps with Bob Forrest, who is a saint for having the compassion and patience to deal with me.

I remember a turning point along my tenuous road to recovery when he finally got tired of my blustering and bullshit and called me out on it.

"You talk about drugs all the time," he said. "Nonstop."

I nodded. "Yeah, because I love them. I miss them. I want to do them. This sucks."

Bob had to keep things very simple and straightforward with me because I'm not that bright. I wasn't going to figure anything out on my own.

"Go get a pen and paper," he said. "Write down the top ten things you want, the ten most important things that will make your life meaningful."

"Meaningful?"

"What would make your life amazing? Incredible? Write down the top ten things you can think of."

Now, I'm not bright, but I wasn't dumb enough to list crack, cocaine, and heroin as the top three things on that list, even though if I'd had that trio the rest of the list could go straight to hell.

So I wrote:

1. A family
2. A girlfriend
3. A career
4. Write a book

5. Finish my record
6. Money
7. Live near the beach
8. Own a home

9. Be happy
10. Have a bunch of really awesome friends

When I was done he said, "Now draw a line next to that list, so you have two columns. In the second column, write down everything on that list you can still have and will most likely get if you go back to getting high."

I said, "What the hell, man? That's a trick."

He said, "No, it's not. Write it down. If you go back to getting high, you're gonna have money? Are you gonna have a family? Are you gonna write a book or have a career? Are you?"

"This is bullshit. You know the answer to that."

He nodded. "I do. And so do you. So shut the fuck up about how much you want to get high."

So I had to get extremely clear on who I was and what I wanted.

Did I want a girlfriend, and hopefully, eventually, a wife and family, or did I want to be a disgusting, junked-out drug addict with scabs on my face?

Because I couldn't have both.

Some of the things were absolutely materialistic, and I had to accept the fact that I can be a very materialistic person.

Did I want to sleep on soft, clean, organic linen sheets, or did I want to crash in Skid Row motels, alleys, and jail cells?

Because I couldn't have both.

Did I want to put my feet in warm sand, feel the breeze on my face, and swim in turquoise waters, or did I want to sit inside blacked-out rooms all day and miss all of it?

I couldn't have both.

I didn't know it at the time, but I was also making this decision:

Did I want to be a selfish addict who sucks everything and everyone around me dry until I finally die, or did I want to stay clean and continue to change so I could go on to create an amazing life and help others do the same?

Knowing that you are holding this book and reading these words, and that they just might help you, feels better than any drug in the world.

I'm not gonna lie, drugs feel really good.

But being really successful, happy, and helping others feels much better. And it's more sustainable.

"I'm often mislabeled as confident. I am rarely confident—in fact I am quite often scared as hell—but I am determined."

— KHALIL RAFATI

Ghost

After the wheels came off, after things got past the point of no return, I began to behave incredibly carelessly and stupid.

Granted, I was a heroin addict and smoking crack every day, so I guess I was already careless and stupid. But once I lost everything and wound up homeless, I began behaving in ways that jeopardized my life to such a degree that when I think back on it now I physically convulse.

I would walk around downtown L.A. flashing cash, sometimes large amounts.

I didn't care.

I just wanted my drugs and I wanted them immediately, so I figured flashing the cash would motivate people.

One night, I was on the move searching for some crack. I was at 5th and Spring and I approached a small group of young black men, asking them if they had any rocks for sale.

Their eyes lit up in the night and they immediately reassured me that yes, in fact they did have lots of crack, and it was good shit too, it was 'Cabbie'.

Cabbie was a slang term used back then to describe high-end crack cocaine. Its origin came from the word caviar, but somehow the V was lost and replaced by B.

They began walking and I followed. We took a right into an alley, then another right, completely blocking us from the street. Then three more guys came out of the shadows and I realized I was about to get bundled.

The idea of getting beaten down obviously scared me, but the fear I had all the way down in my stomach wasn't about getting hurt—I was absolutely certain I was about to die.

This was game over, lights out.

And death, to be honest, wasn't something I cared about until very recently, when I actually did die.

A few weeks prior to that night I had overdosed and flatlined on a friend's kitchen floor. The EMTs brought me back and saved my life.

Since that moment, death terrified me.

In that alley, I could taste the fear in my mouth.

Death was upon me.

Another black man stepped out of the shadows. He was tall and lean and looked to be in his early thirties.

He looked at me, then at the men surrounding me.

He said, "Fuck you doin?"

The men around me looked shaken.

The man barked, "Get the fuck outta here!"

They scattered like mice!

He stepped closer to me.

"You okay?"

I shook my head. In fact, my whole body was shaking.

I was not okay.

I asked him, "Who are you?"

"Ghost," he said. "Why you shaking?"

"I'm sick. I need to get well."

Which meant I needed drugs.

"C'mon," he said.

He started walking. I struggled to keep up with his long strides. He walked with such confidence, and I noticed people moving out of his way as he approached. His clothing didn't quite match our shabby surroundings. They were too nice, too clean.

We walked all the way to the Holiday Inn over by 11th and Hill. He went straight in without a care in the world and the security guard just nodded at him.

Ghost glanced back and told the guard, "He's with me."

We walked into the bathroom and he pulled out a clean rig, still hermetically sealed, and handed me a balloon.

He walked into a stall and fixed and I went into my own and did the same.

I knew what would come next but I didn't care.

At least he was clean and he was nice.

Hopefully he'd finish quickly.

He came out of his stall with that carefree look on his face, the one only a junkie could understand.

"Let's go," he said.

I was stunned.

"You don't need me to do something?"

He said, "Fuck you talking about? I ain't no faggot, are you?"

"No, I just thought..."

"You just thought what?"

Then he laughed and said, "Let's go."

We walked all over downtown L.A. that night for hours. We walked as the sun began to rise. People seemed to know him everywhere. He lectured me on how stupid I was to go into that alley alone, and continued to lecture me on the rules of the street.

I asked him several times why his name was Ghost, but he never answered. Every now and then we would stop off somewhere and go inside and smoke some rock and fix.

Over the next few weeks we developed quite a bond, but I never found out why he was in the alley that first night and he was always vague about who he was, where he came from, and what he did.

He would just show up from time to time, smile at me, and we would take walks and get high. He always had money and dope.

He must have gotten sick of me asking me why his name was Ghost, because one day he said, "Aaron. My real name is Aaron but no one knows that. They all call me Ghost."

Then one day he disappeared.

Just like that.

Gone.

I never got to thank him. I had no idea how to find him. I asked around and people looked at me like I was crazy, like they had no idea who I was talking about.

Many years later, long into my sobriety I had a dream.

I was driving down a very busy street and there he was.

"Ghost!" I yelled.

"Ghost! Ghost!"

He didn't move.

I yelled, "Aaron! Aaron!"

He spun around. It was him! He had this glow to him. He lit up with that smile of his—the invulnerable smile of someone high on dope.

He nodded at me and I woke up, completely out of breath.

"Aaron," I said in the empty room.

Then I began to cry.

What is Sobriety?

Sobriety is building self-esteem.

It's finding humility.

It's finding a relationship with my creator and co-creating a life beyond my wildest dreams full of deep meaning, happiness, joy, and service to others.

No one seems to ask me anymore if I miss drinking or drugs. I used to get asked all the time. I don't regret the past but I will say being clean and sober is 10,000 times better!

The purpose of this life is to live your dreams and realize your destiny. I could never do that when I was drunk and high. Not even close. I wasted years of my life self-medicating, lying to myself while life passed me by.

I was always angry and blaming others for my problems, never taking responsibility for my actions.

Thank you God for my willingness to surrender and join the winning team of life!

Renewal

Soon after the devastating 2018 Woolsey Fire I took a long walk in my favorite canyon with a dear friend. I was hesitant because I knew it had been absolutely destroyed by the fires, but I needed to go. I needed to return to the sacred ground no matter what the condition.

We walked in silence, speechless from the power and fury of the massive fire. The landscape was a mixture of scorched, damp earth and tons of fresh new greenery. The bright green sprouts made me smile, but the loss of all the trees took my breath away. As we walked deeper into the canyon what was left of the trees looked like something out of a Tim Burton film. They were so blackened and twisted they seemed cartoonish.

When I couldn't take it anymore I said, "I hope these trees come back to life."

Then we turned around to walk back. I had a lump in my throat as we walked in silence. Then the vibrant green grass and newly sprouted seedlings began to whisper to me, "Life returns, life is eternal, everything is God, everything is energy!"

I thought of my mother, who was slowly leaving this realm of existence. I thought of the Super Blood Wolf Moon that had eclipsed the previous night.

I thought of the kind and loving man named Jamie who was doing the electrical work on my new house. Right before I left for the hike he stopped by with a housewarming gift. Jamie lost everything in the fire, I mean everything! And yet he offered me a gift, a ridiculously huge agate stone that had to weigh at least twenty pounds. Agates are very rare and one that size is unheard of. And Jamie offered it to me because he knew I would love it.

We kept walking in the canyon and I thought, *We are good, God is great and life is so beautiful!*

Then I saw this tree off in the distance.

I blinked a couple times because it looked like it had green shoots growing out of it. We quickened our pace, crossing a new creek bed the recent rains created, and there it was!

Life blossoming forth!

I burst into tears. It was so perfect.

Our bodies and lives can be destroyed, reduced to charred vessels by the scorched earth oppression of our own egos. Yet our souls are always ready to blossom with new beginnings, if we have the humility to let them.

From the dirt and mud grows the beautiful flower! I love the symbolism in this!

Look how God/nature whispers in our ears. With true faith in God and determination we can turn our darkest times into beautiful ones.

I took this photo in front of the incredible Andaz Maui at Wailea Resort, my all-time favorite hotel.

We are inherently good.

You are inherently good.

"Everything seems futile here except the sun, our kisses, and the wild scents of the earth....Here, I leave order and moderation to others. The great free love of nature and the sea absorbs me completely."

—ALBERT CAMUS

Another Drink

I haven't had a sip of alcohol since 2003. Will I ever take another drink? I wholeheartedly believe I could.

I have healed many, if not most, of the demons I had while I was drinking. I am no longer a tormented soul full of anguish and regrets.

I am completely confident that if I wanted to have a glass of wine, or a bottle of beer, or hell, smoke a joint with a friend, I could do it and have zero problems.

I wouldn't tumble face-first off the wagon into a spiral of self-destruction.

Then why don't I have a drink? It's a three part answer.

First: What if I'm wrong?

What if this seemingly rational opinion is nothing more than my ego trying to trick me into a devastating and horrific set of circumstances?

Most people think of ego as puffing out your chest and carrying around an attitude of superiority, but that is only one part of the ego. The ego is equally about self-loathing and feeling inferior. It is our psychology built on past conditioning.

The ego is like a small child that lives inside of us. It is never satisfied and constantly judges us and everything around us, usually with a negative connotation. When the ego encounters another person, it tries to convince you that you are either superior or inferior to them. There is no gray area, and no equality for the ego.

The ego is the voice inside your head that tells you you're a piece of shit and a loser, or that everyone else is a piece of shit and a loser and you are better than them.

Second: What would I gain?

What real value will drinking or drugs bring into my life at this point? I'm not gonna lie and say it wouldn't be fun to go take a drive out to Joshua Tree with my girlfriend and eat some mushrooms. I'm sure it would be a blast.

But would it be worth risking everything I have now? Would having a glass of wine here and there with dinner bring any amount of tangible or quantifiable value to my life and to those around me? The answer is no. Bottom line, it's just not worth it.

I had my fun. I got away with shit that would've put me in prison for a long, long time. How many times did I drive drunk or high, how many drug deals did I do, how many laws did I break while intoxicated and high? I consumed enough hardcore drugs in the last three or four years of my using to kill an army, yet I am still standing. I am alive and I am healthy and I am free!

I have nothing to gain from alcohol and drugs. They offer me nothing better than what I already have.

Third, and perhaps most important: What if I actually pulled it off?

What if I am now able to drink and use drugs casually or socially? What kind of message would that send to my close, close friends who I love so much, who either didn't have as much time as me, or haven't healed their wounds yet, or haven't had the type of success I've had?

What would happen to them? I am not exactly shy about my actions and achievements. I am not a private person. I'm out in public every day, interacting with hundreds of people in my shops and sometimes hundreds of thousands of people a day on social media or newspaper or TV.

What about all the strangers out there who have read *I Forgot to Die* and say it changed their life? **Saved** their life? Maybe they shouldn't get within a hundred yards of drugs and alcohol, but there I am posting photos of me drinking champagne or toasting with wine, and they think, "Well, if he can do it..."

I don't want to be presumptuous, but I feel like I have a responsibility to my friends and neighbors, to society as a whole.

So could I take another drink and be totally fine?

I definitely don't feel the need to find out.

MY TYPICAL DAY

I get asked pretty regularly about my daily regimen. What I eat, what I drink, supplements, workout routines, sleep habits, and so on. I'm happy to share whatever they want to know, but I have to preface it with a disclaimer.

I'll do the same here:

> My days are based on sixteen years of trial and error.
>
> Some of this won't work for you. Maybe none of it.
>
> If you ask me tomorrow, some of it might be different.
>
> But if you can take one thing from my day and benefit from it, we're off to a good start.

Once you know yourself and really get dialed in with your body and how it responds to various nutrients, sunlight dosage, hydration, sleep, toxins, etc.; you will know what needs to be consistent and what can be modified. For example, do I use animal- or plant-based protein powder? The answer—and I'll expand on this—is that it depends.

> Quick Note: Whenever possible, I've listed my go-to and favorite products at khalilrafati.com/groceries. This list is constantly evolving as I discover new products and what works best for me.

So here's my typical day, more or less:

I wake up without an alarm clock between 5:30 and 6:30 a.m.

See, we might already be off the rails for what works for you. If you have kids, an early work shift, or a crazy long commute you probably think you can't wake up slowly and naturally when your body is ready to. You can, you just need to go to bed earlier.

I know, your shows are on, the game is on, you want to binge a few more episodes of Ozark or Billions.

As with everything, it comes down to what you want. Do you want to stay up late and kickstart your day with a nice fight-or-flight response to your alarm, or do you want to get the rest and recovery your body needs and allow your resting heart rate to lower enough so you not only get enough REM sleep, you get enough deep sleep as well. Both are critically important for recovery and rejuvenation. I use an Oura ring to track all of this.

After I wake up I immediately go into the bathroom and spray my face with organic rose water because of what it does for my skin and what it does for my spirit. I drink sixteen ounces of Mountain Valley water, many times with a pinch of Premier Research Laboratories Pink Himalayan Sea Salt and the juice from half a lemon. For whatever reason I've always been the guy who literally stops to smell the roses, and rose water really resonates with me.

Morning Coffee

Then I prepare and drink three shots of espresso or French press coffee to clear out the night's cobwebs. I use Papua New Guinea or Ethiopian beans. The coffee gives me energy as well as mental clarity, and it also staves off my hunger so my body can continue to enjoy the benefits of intermittent fasting, which started around 6 p.m. after my last meal the previous evening.

If I'm traveling or if I have a lot of writing to do I will forego my straight black coffee and add Four Sigmatic's chaga mushroom blend, a packet of organic Stevia, some brain octane or MCT oil and some heavy whipping cream.

By this point it's usually around six or six-thirty in the morning, everything around me is still quiet, and I prepare for a very short, intense period during which I accomplish the best work of the day. This is when I make the most progress toward my goal of that moment. Maybe it's creating a new recipe, or finding the purest source of organic acai berries, or researching which nutrients will take one of Sun-Life's products over the top for our customers.

Everybody is different. If your energy for flow state, deep work, whatever you want to call it, is more aligned with mid-day, or evening, or two a.m., find a way to get it done. This is when you make exponential progress toward your goals. Do it for one hour after you wake up. Or one hour before you go to bed. If you can handle it, do both.

Walk

I take a walk outside every day, regardless of the weather. (I live in Malibu, so that isn't as tough as it may sound.) I love watching the sun come up, and that quiet time between me, the earth, and my creator is vital. It primes me for when I'm ready to head back inside for some deeply creative work.

My Flow State Environment

I'm a fragrance guy. My work area has a diffuser going with whatever essential oils are working for me at the time, like rosemary, frankincense, or blue spruce. My chair is surrounded by crystals so I can feel their energy. The chair is super comfortable for me, and I slap a defender shield on my lap to protect myself from the electromagnetic frequencies from the computer. I put a pillow covered in question marks on top of that with, "There were rules?!" printed on it to fuel my defiance and inspire me. I also have several cashmere blankets to keep the temperature perfect. Then I grab the laptop and get rolling.

The overall result is a little amphitheater, or shrine, to working toward my goals. It's not lost on me that this nearly ceremonial approach to my deep work is similar to an addict's ritual. It's just another habit with different ingredients, different choices, and different goals. Combined, they will greatly impact what life looks like in one year, three years, five years, ten years, twenty years.

What Gets Done in an Hour?

A while back I came across this delicious vegan sorbet, better than any ice cream I've ever tasted, and I had to track down the source. It was a brilliant man who makes it organic, gluten-free and vegan, which isn't a requirement by any means but is great for some customers.

Once I knew I could get the vegan sorbet in quantity from him, I spent one morning creating a recipe around it. I found another source for quinoa crisps sweetened with coconut nectar, and thought, "What if you take this vegan sorbet and you throw these quinoa crisps on top, and then you hit it with some peanut butter and maybe some date syrup? What would that taste like?"

Well, you can come to any SunLife Organics and order the Bali Bowl to find out. I created that recipe in one hour.

Sauna

When I'm done with my deep work I extract myself from the cocoon of laptop, pillow, blanket, and chair and take 200 mg of decaffeinated green tea extract and bitter melon extract.

Then I take a sauna, the benefits of which are truly wonderful. (I get into more sauna details in the next chapter.)

Work

Fueled by an inspiring, productive morning, I get after the rest of the workday. This could mean driving between SunLife locations to handle ownership duties, reviewing new lease opportunities and contracts, meeting with wholesalers, washing blenders, chopping fruit, sweeping patios, weeding flower beds, cleaning toilets—whatever is necessary to best serve my customers and employees, and I do all of it with a smile. None of it is work. All of it is an opportunity.

Workout

Twice a week I do a high-intensity interval training circuit in the early afternoon. To mix things up I'll do ten minutes of walking or rowing alternating with ten minutes of incline walking, followed by ten minutes on the assault bike.

Before the workout I take:

> Five grams of creatine monohydrate, which helps me keep muscle mass and increases strength. It also increases my cognitive function—I think and feel better.
>
> One scoop of an amino acid complex, which optimizes my overall health. Ben Greenfield makes a great version under the Kion brand, and so does Thorne.

Smoothie Time

At 11:00 a.m. every day I have a superfood smoothie or acai bowl (for smoothie and bowl recipes, go to khalilrafati.com/recipes). This meal includes lots of berries:

blueberries, strawberries, raspberries, blackberries, and acai berries, all of which are full of health-promoting polyphenols. I also like to mix in plant-based protein powder, hemp protein powder, pea protein powder, rice protein powder, collagen, and whey protein powder. Try them all and see what works for you.

I sometimes add colostrum, which is a freeze-dried powder made from cow or goat mothers' milk. If you want proof of the fortifying and healing health benefits of colostrum, take a look at a newly born calf. On day one it's spindly and helpless. A few days later, after being nourished with its mother's milk, it's a beautiful and majestic animal jumping and romping around.

Once a week I'll do a free-for-all smoothie including maca, bee pollen, raw royal jelly, aloe juice, hemp milk, lotus pollen, liquid minerals, silica, greens (spinach, kale, or dandelion), all blended together. Sometimes I'll add:

Coconut meat

Butter

Greens powder

Spirulina or chlorella or both

Lotus pollen

Probiotics

Whatever else may be calling out to me

In the smoothie and bowl recipes, and throughout the rest of my diet, you'll see plants, meat, dairy, grains, and just about anything else that can be consumed by a human being. I certainly would not label myself vegan or even vegetarian, although plant-based foods make up 60 to 80 percent of my diet on any given day. Sometimes 100% of my diet is plant-based. Again, I shy away from militant dietary restrictions or labels. I don't feel the need to find my identity through a diet.

I go into more detail about my overall nutrition in the next chapter.

Dinner

I usually wrap work around 5, ready for a light dinner of some sort of grass-fed, pasture-raised, or wild unprocessed protein and a green vegetable. I typically go for fish, chicken, beef, or lamb with a lightly dressed salad of healthy greens. After 6 p.m. I don't eat or drink anything else for the rest of the day except water. Sometimes if I'm feeling reckless and crazy I'll have sparkling water with lemon.

Inspiration

The next part of my day is where a lot of people struggle. What you do between dinner and bedtime is key for achieving your goals across all domains. This is where you can really increase and reinforce the benefits of the changes you're making in your life.

It's very easy to choose something that will turn my brain off and provide empty entertainment for a couple hours before heading to bed. And I indulge every now and then, especially if my girlfriend and I have discovered a great series and we can't wait to huddle up on the couch to see what happens next.

But the majority of the time I choose a bookend for my morning deep work. If I'm going to watch something, I choose a documentary about a subject that is fascinating me or inspirational videos that fire me up for the next day. Or I'll jump on YouTube and watch a Joe Rogan podcast. For some reason, his podcasts are much more interesting to watch than listen to, probably because he's so animated and such an amazing color commentator. Sometimes I'll sit with my eyes closed and listen to an audiobook.

All of these plant seeds that will grow into ideas, action, and change.

Sacred Sleep

Sleep is sacred and the most important component for healing, recovery and rejuvenation. I go to bed between 9 and 9:30 p.m. every night in a completely blacked-out bedroom, a space I consider my sanctuary. The only items in my room are a 100% certified organic latex mattress with a Chilly Pad, a nightstand with several spiritual/inspirational books, a couple of giant crystals on both sides of the bed, and a dresser with the complete volume of The Zohar bookended by two more giant crystals. I also have several massive plants to surround myself with living things producing fresh oxygen and a Molekule air purifier that is always on.

The entire room is electromagnetic field (EMF)-proofed with Geovital paint grounded to the electrical outlets. Underneath the natural oak floor is a heavy layer of mesh that blocks any dirty electricity and EMFs.

Why do I go to bed so early? So I can wake up naturally the next morning before sunrise and start all over again. I don't think of sleep as recovering from today—I think of it as preparing for tomorrow.

Boring is Beautiful.

Please do not be fooled by my personal Instagram profile.

These are not my private jets.

I drive a Volvo.

These are definitely not my penthouses. I live in a modest townhouse.

Even the fancy vacations are not mine. I am a grateful invited guest.

I make smoothies for a living.

Most days you can find me washing blenders at one of my shops or picking up trash out front or tending to the plants.

I don't go out.

I don't go to clubs.

I don't go to parties.

I go to bed at 9 o'clock at night and wake up at 5:30 in the morning.

I eat dinner at 5 p.m. every night and most nights I eat alone.

I am incredibly boring and couldn't be happier!

I travel a lot, usually alone.

I need to be bored. Bored is so good for me. All of my great ideas come to me when I am bored. Daily rituals and routines tend to stifle my creative juices, especially if I cling to them too tightly.

"Can you sit still long enough until your mud settles and your water becomes clear?"

— LAO TZU, TAO TE CHING

The Perfect Day

Breathe

Meditate

Dream

Visualize

Believe

Create

Smile

Laugh

Love

Be kind

Pray and give thanks

Wake up tomorrow and repeat

Every Day Counts

Make every day count, make every action count.

Find your purpose and make sure each action brings you more in line with your purpose.

If what you are doing habitually doesn't serve you or others, take a break from it and try something new.

"Figure out some way to get paid to play."

— ALAN WATTS

Most people don't realize they have a body until it's too late. That's why you see all of these 50-year-old guys completely out of shape riding $14,000 racing bikes up and down the Pacific Coast Highway in skin-tight biker shorts with freshly shaved legs.

They worked their asses off in a career they hated and are stuck in relationships with women who have contempt for them, but they are bound by societal, religious or financial confines so they stay in their self-imposed prisons until one day they wake up and realize they have a body that they've been drastically neglecting and it is about to give out on them.

Buying something expensive like a bike because all their friends are doing it is easy. Getting back on a bicycle for the first time in forty years probably feels really good and reminds them of the innocence of their youth.

So they grab some biker shorts, shave their legs, and head out in packs of twelve to fifteen where they ride for twenty miles, developing severe butt rash and stopping off at every Starbucks along the way to suck down a venti Frappuccino loaded with 400 milligrams of caffeine and 23 teaspoons of table sugar.

It doesn't make sense...but it totally makes sense.

They've been sitting in chairs for the last thirty-five years, one of the worst things you can do for the human body. Once they begin to engage their legs and glutes through bicycling they experience a surge in testosterone, which makes them feel alive again. So I totally understand it.

It's just really sad when you see these guys walking around in their $400 clip-on bicycle shoes with their duck butts sticking out from compressed discs in their lower back and their giant abdomens with skinny little stick legs and fat, old man faces, bloated from the gluten, sugar, and yeast in alcohol.

When I moved here in 1992 I was absolutely fucking blown away that all of these bloated old men would risk their lives every Saturday and Sunday riding up and down PCH. I had to figure out why so I started to pay attention and all of this came to me.

We are animals and we are creatures of habit. Yes, we are self-aware which differentiates us from all other living things according to the best science available. But we are still animals and creatures of habit. Therefore, whatever habits we establish by mimicking the actions of our peer group will ultimately define where we end up later in life.

You become who you hang out with. No negotiating that.

You imitate your environment. No negotiating that.

Whatever you read, whatever you listen to, whatever you watch is exactly what you will become.

Most people on the planet will live lives of quiet desperation. I beg you to not make this mistake.

The Luxury of Alone

I love to rest and be alone.

I love to get away for a few days and lay low, not speak, lay in bed all day, order room service and take multiple naps.

Rest and solitude are rarely discussed and highly, highly underrated.

"The unexamined life is not worth living," and no better way for introspection than solitude.

Ojai is absolutely magical and these grounds are reverberating with healing life force! The air is so clean, the trees so alive. I woke up to the bluest of blue skies this morning and saw snow on the mountains off in the distance.

I walked past these aloe plants on the way to the spa and had to snap a photo.

Thank you God for this incredible life.

Thank you, God for the elimination of the massive amount of cognitive dissonance that has been lifted.

One of my biggest fears used to be being alone; now it's one of my greatest luxuries!

Self Can't Reveal Self to Self

That is absolutely not true.

I mean it's true if you are suffering from untreated alcoholism and your head is on fire with lust, resentment, jealousy, and so on. If that's the case then yes, it's going to be very difficult to observe yourself honestly.

But when you have a job and you are making a decent living and treating people kindly and making a solid effort to be the person that God intended you to be, it is not that difficult to observe yourself.

Sobriety. Eating right, meditating, exercising moderately, praying throughout the day, thinking loving thoughts and being kind. For me, this is the only way to live.

This is considered the straight and narrow, but there is nothing straight or narrow about it.

It can create massive opportunities and abundance and prosperity. Financial freedom, a quiet mind, and loving friendships with amazing people.

NUTRITION: PUT GOOD FOOD INTO YOUR BODY

Keep it Simple

Let's start with the basics. It is very easy—and marketers know this—to get caught up in the latest fads, technologies and supplements.

Keep it simple.

Stop eating anything that isn't an animal, vegetable, fruit, nut, or seed in its natural, unprocessed state.

Drink a liter of water with salt and a freshly squeezed lemon or lime as soon as you wake up. The citrus juice is packed with vitamin C, has detoxifying and antibacterial properties, and will support healthy digestion and metabolism.

Go for a walk every day.

Deep inhalations through your nose and deep exhalations through your mouth.

A walking gratitude list or a simple prayer:

"Good morning, God. Thank you for this day. Thank you for this perfect health. Thank you for this perfect wealth. Thank you for this perfect love."

Start with those simple things and your life will improve drastically.

The key here is consistency.

Habits.

If you give yourself wiggle room, you're going to wiggle.

You'll feel the pull to get distracted by fancy supplements and so-called biohacks. Ignore them. Until you've realized your full natural potential through consistent lifestyle habits around food, water, movement, breathing and gratitude, you shouldn't worry about additions.

Subtract and simplify first.

Add and complicate later if you need to...but you probably won't.

In fact, let's start now. Take a deep breath in through your nose, hold it until you're done reading this part, and exhale through parted lips.

Thank your creator for the opportunity to take that breath.

You're off to a great start.

Calm down.

You are sufficient.

"This is my wish for you: Comfort on difficult days, smiles when sadness intrudes, rainbows to follow the clouds, laughter to kiss your lips, sunsets to warm your heart, hugs when spirits sag, beauty for your eyes to see, friendships to brighten your being, faith so that you can believe, confidence for when you doubt, courage to know yourself, patience to accept the truth, Love to complete your life."

—RALPH WALDO EMERSON

A big shift came when I read the book *The Power of Habit* by Charles Duhig.

The truth is I only read the first third of the book because a lot of it was over my head.

But it had such a profound impact on me that I really started to scrutinize some habits I had that most definitely were not serving me, and I was absolutely fascinated by how ingrained they were in my daily life and how much resistance I came up against when I tried to change them.

It was so blatantly obvious, even after only a quick glance under the hood, of how these seemingly insignificant habits were not just negatively impacting my life but really robbing me of the opportunity to reach my highest potential.

Another strange little piece of wisdom came to me when I was listening to the

Tim Ferriss podcast with Ramit Sethi. They were talking about how he woke up every single day, seven days a week, and exercised for only 10 minutes. I'm paraphrasing and it could've been 12 minutes, but the point was that he did it every single day and never thought about it and he found that approach to be incredibly beneficial.

I was one of those guys who went to the gym and somehow managed to spend a couple of hours there, if not more. The problem with that is that my life became so busy that going to the gym started to become not impossible but definitely not practical; so I went less and less.

Same thing with yoga. Even though the yoga class was an hour and fifteen minutes it somehow took three hours out of my day.

I have a very strong tendency to, as my girlfriend says, "dillydally." I am the king of dillydallying!

So I took what I learned in the first few chapters of *The Power of Habit* and also what Ramit said about his workouts, and I started to apply it to my life.

I found it strangely easy—in fact almost effortless—to bring these new habits into my life and they very quickly replaced some old habits.

About three months later, people started to compliment me on my physical appearance and told me I seemed much more confident, much more grounded.

And all I had done was commit to a few simple things:

The first thing is I started taking a twenty minute walk in the morning and that alone seemed to really shift things for me.

Sometimes I walk longer—thirty or forty minutes—but the point is I committed to taking a walk every morning.

Because of this my body feels and looks better and my mind is less cluttered. Most days when I'm alone I do a walking gratitude list. I start really simple, like a roof over my head and clean water to bathe in and to drink, and then I begin to dive a little bit deeper into gratitude.

Many times my gratitude becomes so big I will literally start saying out loud, "Thank you God, thank you thank you thank you!!!"

Some days my girlfriend joins me, and that's a whole other level of happiness and intimacy. She's really quiet and we usually don't say much on our walks, and yet somehow in that silence we seem to say more to one another than most conversations I've ever had with other people.

There is a peace and comfort there, and a certain knowing that leaves me filled with confidence and joy.

Secondly, I made a decision to not eat my first meal until 11 a.m. I get up in the morning and have a cup of coffee and that's it.

I remember being nervous when I first made the commitment, and yet the following day it was almost effortless. A couple of times I felt a little hungry, but I just drank some water and that was it.

The third thing I committed to, I have to be honest, was a little bit more challenging and took a while to establish: I made a commitment to not eat anything after seven p.m.

I have been a night snacker for as long as I can remember, and the problem is the snacks at night were not the good kind or the kind that served my body.

I went back and forth the first couple of weeks and kept coming up against a lot of resistance. In the end, the solution was actually pretty black-and-white: I had to throw everything out.

And I mean *everything*.

Popcorn, chips, trail mix, pretty much anything that I could snack on and rationalize, minimize, and justify. And lo and behold, once there was nothing to snack on I stopped snacking!

Over the years I have definitely had some covert trips to the gas station to buy a bag of Doritos or somehow manipulated my girlfriend into joining me for a giant bowl of popcorn drenched in butter and salt, but for the most part I eat a big dinner around 5 p.m. and then I treat myself to a bag of Siete Nacho flavored chips.

I always have three or four bags of Siete chips in my cabinet. I feel that allowing myself to binge on them after my last meal is a very healthy and happy compromise.

I am in the greatest shape of my life now as a result of these three habits. I still go to the gym sometimes but I limit myself to 20 minutes. A quick warm-up on the Assault AirBike and a couple of rounds of a HIIT workout and that's it.

As far as yoga or stretching, I now do that in my far infrared sauna while listening to audiobooks so I get to do three things at once with little or no effort. While everyone else is still sleeping or hitting snooze for the fourth time, I am detoxing my body, optimizing my hormones, educating myself and staying supple and limber like a brand new baby boy!

Do I still struggle?

Do I still have habits that aren't serving me?

Yes, of course.

This is progress, not perfection.

I always wanted to build Rome in a day or sprint up to the top of Mount Everest, but shit doesn't work like that.

I am the personification of a late bloomer and still, as I have mentioned before, a deeply flawed human being with lots of character defects and shortcomings.

Laziness and procrastination have haunted me my entire life. In my younger days during those godless winters in Ohio I became a world champion at laying on the sofa in the fetal position, watching TV and feeling sorry for myself.

Over the years I have consciously and subconsciously set myself up for failure.

Failure is familiar, and failure always allowed me to have excuses about how unfair life was and how everyone else was so lucky.

Everyone else seemed to be able to get up on time and not sleep through their alarm clocks.

Everyone else got good grades and stayed out of trouble.

Everyone else seemed naturally gifted and good at sports.

Everyone else had great parents that love them, blah blah blah blah!

I could never get up in the morning.

I always had bad grades.

I was terrible at sports.

I was always in trouble and in the principal's office.

I was told by my teachers that I was bad, that I was stupid.

I was told by my coaches that I was lazy and talentless.

Even worse, I was told by my own father over and over again that I was a piece of shit.

That I was stupid.

That I was a bum.

His favorite thing to scream at me was, "You're a goddamn idiot, you're a goddamn prima donna whore!"

The volume and timber of his voice was crippling and his words always left me shattered and confused. All I wanted was for this man to love me. All I wanted was his love and approval and yet somehow I always got the opposite.

I felt those experiences, along with a bunch of other traumatic shit, gave me free reign to behave selfishly and carelessly throughout my childhood and into early adulthood. The problem is, I continued on.

There is nothing okay about behaving the way that I did once I hit my mid-twenties.

And the sad, pathetic truth is, I carried on like that well into my early thirties.

I'm so grateful that I finally bottomed out and ran out of options.

In one sense being thirty-three years old, a high school dropout, a convicted felon and a recovering drug addict is a horrible position to find yourself in.

But it's just as easy to assess that situation and realize the only way I could go from there is up with no limits!

These tiny little micro adjustments, these tiny little shifts and behaviors that quickly became habits have radically altered my existence.

From the ashes, debris, rubble and wreckage of my past I was able to move from crawling to standing upright and ultimately find my way to a new life.

A life I never could've dreamed of.

Today I don't just stand upright—I walk forward with absolute certainty.

One of the kids who works at SunLife was laughing and making fun of me when I walked into the store.

I whipped around and said, "What's so funny?"

She said, "The way you walk."

"What's funny about it?"

She said, "You walk like you have armed guards walking behind you."

Don't Shit in the Temple

A couple years ago I was walking out of a CVS Pharmacy when my eyes were drawn to the far corner of the parking lot. Sitting there, all by itself surrounded by an empty sea of parking spots, was a gorgeous matte-green V8 Brabus Mercedes-Benz G-Class.

I mean, this car was immaculate. A dream car. It looked like something James Bond would drive (the Daniel Craig James Bond). The rims and windows were blacked-out, but I could see the outline of the driver inside. I felt compelled to tell him how much I admired this beautiful machine.

But as I approached, I saw a plume of smoke erupt from the driver's window. I winced. It was bad enough to taint the interior of such a pristine automobile, but to—my disapproval was temporarily interrupted when the driver opened the door and got out, crumpling an empty McDonald's bag in his hands. We locked eyes.

"Oh, shit," he said. "Busted."

He was a customer of mine, someone who had struggled with his weight for years. And here he was, putting filth into his lungs and body while sitting inside an immaculately detailed, cleaned, and maintained $60,000 sport utility vehicle.

Would he put garbage in the gas tank of that car?

Would he pump cancerous toxins into the ventilation system? (He already was by smoking in the car, but he didn't see it that way.)

Would he work for hours to make the spotless exterior gleam like a chariot from the heavens, then dump a bunch of shit inside?

No. But that's exactly what he was doing to his own body. He treated his car better than his body. I see it all the time with things: cars, bikes, houses, golf clubs...

Even more so with children and pets. I see toddlers enjoying fresh, mashed-up organic fruits and vegetables while their parents shove processed burgers into their mouths.

Pet owners sit on the patio, and when a potato chip falls on the ground they yell, "No! That will make you sick!" Then they finish the rest of the bag.

We deserve better. My customer in the CVS parking lot knew it, too. He knew that even though his car is certainly a wonderful machine, his body is a miracle. A gift from the source of creation and millions of years of evolution, fighting every second of every day to keep him alive, functioning, healthy.

All of those cells forming and collapsing so he can move, breathe, speak, love, laugh, cry. But they don't have the power to stop him from poisoning himself.

Only he has that power.

We change the oil in our cars regularly. We wash them weekly. We take them in for regular maintenance, and many of us only use premium unleaded. We polish them, vacuum them, detail them, and yet we treat our bodies like garbage dumps. Constantly dumping trash and poison into the only machine that truly matters.

We neglect/abuse the one machine that we literally cannot live without. Processed foods, sugary sodas, high fructose corn syrup, wheat products laden with glyphosate, low-grade water in plastic bottles, artificial light, sitting for hours at a time, going without proper sleep. We have become a nation of domesticated animals bred for taxation and pumped full of pharmaceuticals.

In many ways the movie *The Matrix* has become real. The book *1984* by George Orwell is now a reality and no one seems to notice or care. These aren't conspiracy theories—this is reality! My phone has a GPS, camera and microphone that documents every location, gesture and word I speak. Every time I use Siri to type for me everything I say is being chronicled and stored. There's a camera on my computer and television watching and listening.

Before I go too far down the rabbit hole I want to point out it doesn't have to be this way. We can reclaim our health and become young and vibrant again. We can recapture the energy of our youth and live fully and completely! We can get away from these weird little devices that have taken over our entire lives!

A return to health, a return to youth, a return to an authentic well-lived life full of deep meaning and joy!

Or, we can spend our lives unhealthy and bloated, shuffling toward failure and regret.

But why not make your life a Masterpiece?!

Cowards die many times before their deaths; the valiant taste death but once!

But don't think for a moment it's gonna be easy. If you're of the mindset that posting cute pics of yourself on Instagram will somehow miraculously and instantaneously transform your life into one of abundance and freedom, you are gravely mistaken. There were times in the last sixteen years when I was working seven days a week, sixteen hours a day, sweating like a whore in church. I felt I could no longer go on. But I did. Through lots of trials and tribulations, peaks and valleys, failures and victories. The point is, I just kept going.

That is my only talent. I just don't give up.

Love, Not Labels

After well over a decade of experimenting with every type of diet under the sun, including but not limited to vegetarian, vegan, raw vegan, carnivore, paleo, primal, ancestral, macrobiotic, etc. etc. etc., what I've found is the ultimate and optimal diet for me is a majority of all-organic vegetables and fruits combined with a moderate amount of super-high quality grass-fed, pasture-raised or wild animal proteins.

I augment this diet with quite a few superfoods, medicinal mushrooms, supplements like fish oil, magnesium, various probiotics that I constantly switch up, some amazing green powders, and various tonics and elixirs. I provide a full list at khalilrafati.com.com/supplements.

Given the choice, we should consume 100% organic vegetables and fruits and grass-fed, pasture-raised or wild animal proteins. In other words, things that you eat shouldn't have ingredients. For the most part they should either be an animal or a vegetable.

So what are you?

Vegan or Vegetarian?

Paleo or Primal?

Carnivore or Keto?

The better question is: What story comes with that label for you? It is very easy to form a part of your identity through harsh dietary restrictions. I see this all the time from people at both ends of the vegan/carnivore spectrum. You've probably heard the joke: How can you tell which person at the table is a vegan? You don't have to—they'll tell you.

The same goes for someone who identifies as gluten-free, paleo, whatever. And again, I've been all of these "labels." We somehow convince ourselves that people are actually interested in what we eat and why we don't eat certain things. I wish more people understood that nobody gives a shit, and it's actually quite annoying. Stop taking pictures of your food and say a prayer instead. Give thanks, even if you don't believe in God, because God still loves you either way.

Remember Sarah from *I Forgot to Die*? She was the gnarliest drug addict I'd ever met. She made my story seem tame in comparison. Well, she's stayed off drugs and alcohol for the last ten years and is absolutely more gorgeous than ever. Every year I take a trip with her and her dad around the time of her sober birthday, and one time we spent a month in India together.

On this particular trip her uncle tagged along, and within ten seconds of meeting the guy he started talking about being a vegan. Obviously I wanted to be polite, so I acted interested the first forty-seven times he brought it up.

But as the days rolled on, he began to dominate every conversation, especially during meals. We were all taken hostage for hours at a time while he sat and pontificated on the virtues of veganism. It was nauseating and began to ruin the trip.

On one of our last days in India, as he was rambling on and on through one of his standard vegan diatribes, I finally broke.

I told him, "I get it. That's enough. I don't need to hear any more. I was a vegetarian for eleven years, and the whole time I was hungry and lethargic. I was miserable."

He said, "Well, I've been a vegan now for two months, and I've never felt better."

I almost dove across the table and choked him out.

Of course you're going to feel better if you've only been a vegan for two months! When we make a radical change like that, it's typically out of desperation because we're experiencing some sort of crisis. Sure enough, he had gone to his doctor and received very alarming news: his cholesterol was almost 400. His doctor prescribed him statens and a friend of his bought him a book on veganism. He must have read it five times, because he regurgitated the book's information like it was gospel, written by God himself.

We've all seen this before, right? Someone reads a book, hears a podcast, or watches a documentary on Netflix and all of a sudden they're an expert in that field. And maybe whatever they're doing and preaching about works for them. If so, great.

The point I'm trying to make here is: educate yourself with as many different sources as possible. Make sure you take in a broad spectrum of information. If you're listening to nothing but *Bulletproof Radio*, maybe you should subscribe to Rich Roll's podcast, too. Or, if you want more of an all-encompassing point of view, try Joe Rogan's podcast.

If you've read *The China Study* and are convinced everyone should be a vegan, try reading *Kiss the Ground.*

One of the most interesting and compelling conversations about veganism, vegetarianism and eating animals was The Hidden Cost of Veganism, episode #143 of Daniel Vitalis's podcast *ReWild Yourself.*

Daniel is definitely on the fringe and his podcast is not for everyone, but that particular episode is so incredibly informative, and really helped me understand some of the people I knew and the health struggles they were having as a result of their dogmatic approach to diet.

Again, I'm not telling anyone to eat meat, or to be a vegan. It's not my job to prescribe diets or to save anyone. My duty is to only speak my own personal experience and what works for me and my body.

You need to listen to your own body. I'm just trying to help people avoid as much cognitive bias as possible and avoid deriving a sense of self from some strict diet they read or heard about or witnessed on Netflix.

And as always, the truth most likely lies somewhere in the middle. People eating a ton of meat all the time might benefit from some fruits, vegetables and nuts. And people who are strict vegans might do well incorporating things like grass-fed butter, bone broth, or possibly even small amounts of wild game.

Listen to your body.

Is the food you're consuming really making you as healthy as you can be, or is it a part of your old story? Do you actually thrive from putting butter and oil in your coffee, or do you just like being a part of that tribe?

Don't become a convict of your convictions. Convictions are dangerous and can be detrimental. Since you're already dropping your old story, forget the labels you've been using for your diet and explore everything, just like the hunter gatherer you are.

But if you're going to have convictions about your diet, here are some safe bets:

Avoid all processed foods and sugars.

Avoid artificial sweeteners. Use stevia or monk fruit instead.

Avoid hydrogenated oils, also known as trans fats.

Avoid junk food. You don't need me to tell you what qualifies as junk food—you know it when you see it.

Just eat clean.

Eat organic.

Eat vegetables, fruits and animals.

If you don't want to eat animals, that's fine, just don't starve yourself or cause serious health problems because of it.

And if you don't want to eat animals because you don't want them to die, I think that is beautiful. But unfortunately they are going to die anyway, and so are you and I, and at the end of the day me living to my highest potential, serving my community and being the man that God intended me to be comes first before everything.

While we obsess about paleo, primal, keto, gluten-free, vegan, carnivore, ancestral diets and trends, the rest of the world has breakfast.

We have gyms and sports clubs and Pilates studios and spin cycle studios on every corner, but I don't see those anywhere when I travel to other countries.

Only in L.A. will people sit around and talk about how fruit is bad for you.

Money is Not an Excuse

You don't have to be rich to eat nutritious food. I was talking with an employee about how delicious grass-fed beef and wild bacon tastes, and she said, "Oh, yeah. I know I need to eat like that, but I don't spend my money on the good stuff."

I said, "You need to."

"Yeah, I know. I know."

And maybe she did, but she didn't want to do it. Maybe she was like me running away from yoga—she knew it was the right thing to do but had cognitive dissonance between the evidence and the action.

After our conversation I happened to be at the grocery store and I decided to get her stocked up on what she knew she should be eating. My hope was that she would feel so amazing she would never go back to eating empty calories and processed junk all the time.

I also wanted to show her the receipt to prove she could eat that way all the time.

The steps were pretty simple:

1. Get a blender. A cheap one if you have to, a better one if you can.
2. Go to the grocery store and get a giant bag of organic pre-washed greens. Spinach, kale, or chard, whatever you prefer, and mix it all up. You can stick the whole bag in your freezer if you can't get through it before it goes mushy.
3. Get bags of frozen organic berries, whatever kind you like.
4. Get a tub or bag of organic protein powder.
5. Get some organic powdered superfoods/greens.
6. Go home and put those ingredients in a blender with organic apple juice, hemp milk, or water.
7. Drink it.
8. Repeat.

You can also get grass-fed and organic meat from Costco in bulk quantities, but if you have the money find a farm like Belcampo. Cook it all up on Sunday night for a week of meals with your super greens, or freeze it and prepare as needed.

If you have access to a farmers market or Community Supported Agriculture (CSA), you can get more fresh, local produce than you'll know what to do with, and the little money you spend gets to stay in your community.

Bottom line: Money is not an excuse to eat like shit.

For more of my preferred food sources,
check out khalilrafati.com/groceries.

There are no shortcuts.

There are no free lunches.

There are no magic pills.

There are no supplements that will make you "limitless."

You don't need to hack anything.

And diets don't work.

This topic is especially frustrating to me because of my personal experience with change. I made a couple of little tweaks in my habits and food choices, and I am in the best shape of my life by far!

People ask me all the time about how many calories are in my smoothies and bowls. How much fat? How many carbs?

It doesn't matter. These are the wrong questions. Everything we serve is incredibly nutrient-dense and organic. You could eat ten of my bowls a day and you'd lose fat and feel amazing.

But this isn't a sales pitch. I'm not telling you this to promote anything except common sense and your own good health.

People are fighting an endless, needless battle of counting calories, cutting fat and adding cardio. The treadmills and ellipticals they use are, ironically, the perfect metaphor. You can run and ride on them all day and literally get **nowhere**.

It is simple.

Eat vegetables, fruits and animals. Or just vegetables and fruits.

Skip the sugar and processed wheat.

Eat **food**. Food doesn't come in a box with an expiration date three years from now.

This is a simple change that is not sexy, not flashy, and won't make anyone in the health and wellness industry rich.

But it will make you healthier. It will get you closer to being well.

It is one vital step toward being the best version of yourself.

Spring Detox

(Again, I am not a doctor. I just do what works for me—proceed at your own risk.)

Every spring I do a three-, five-, or seven-day bowel detox. Out with the old, in with the new, right?

Go to your favorite health food store and see what kind of bowel detoxifier they have. Then see if it works for you. As before, I am simply mentioning what works for me.

I'm an addict addicted to healthy things! So much better than when I was using the bad stuff.

Try intermittent fasting by taking a fourteen to sixteen hour break in between your last meal of the day and your first meal of the next. I am pretty rigid about this, and ninety percent of the time I eat dinner between 5 and 6 p.m. and I won't eat again until 11 a.m. the following day.

I do, however, drink black coffee when I wake up between 5:30 and 6 a.m.. This doesn't seem to mess with my fast.

Do some form of light exercise every day, even if you start with only five minutes.

Experiment with different supplements—being careful not to overdo it—and see what works for you.

And if you haven't already, introduce probiotics to your body. Gut health is absolutely paramount to overall health.

Supplements

I take many different supplements depending on the time of year, how I'm feeling, and the current demands on my body and mind. Because this information is constantly changing, I have an up-to-date list with information on each supplement at khalilrafati.com/supplements, but I do want to cover two of them here because I think they're that important.

What Goes On Your Body Goes In Your Body

If I won't put it in my body, I won't put it on my body.

What do you think happens to those lotions, creams, and cosmetics you rub all over? It says right there on the label: Ultra-Absorption, Hydrating, Moisturizing. They soak into your skin, where they are free to enter your bloodstream. Cosmetic companies have been busted for using chemicals like formaldehyde and asbestos in their products, and I'm willing to bet the other ingredients aren't much better.

Would I eat formaldehyde and asbestos? Hell no.

Would I eat fluoride, which is more toxic than lead? No, that's why I won't allow it in my toothpaste or water.

Would I eat aluminum and nickel? No, that's why I won't allow them in my deodorant. Does it sound like a good idea to slather toxic chemicals under your arm, then clamp down, helping them soak in right next to the axillary artery and vein, which carry blood to and from your abdomen and arms?

And that's just for deodorant—don't even mention antiperspirant. If you deliberately block your body from getting rid of toxins and mess with its heating and cooling system by denying it a major outlet for sweat, you're asking for trouble.

So what's the solution? Miraculous coconut oil will handle just about all of this. With coconut oil you can:

Mix in your favorite essential oils for a scented, toxin-free skin moisturizer and hair pomade with natural antioxidants

Detoxify your teeth and gums

Mix in baking soda to make a toothpaste and deodorant

Shave

Soothe sunburn

You can also use natural shea butter as a moisturizer, pomade, shave butter and gentle sunscreen.

The best part about both of these: you can literally grab a spoon and eat both of them and they will make you healthier. Look at the label on any manufactured beauty product and it will scream, "If you ingest this, call the poison hotline immediately!" I mean, they're flat-out telling us to avoid these products altogether, we just don't listen.

Get a tub of coconut oil or shea butter while you're stocking up at Costco. It will last you for months, if not longer, and you won't be putting anything on—or in—your body that will try to kill you.

I also have a list of recommended toxin-free products at khalilrafati.com/beauty.

Every 18 months there's a new diet starting. In the early 90s I was introduced to 40/40/20 diet, or whatever it was called, and everybody went crazy about it, talking about it nonstop. Then there was the Atkins diet which also took the nation by storm.

Then came the raw food diet, so everyone stopped eating animal products and only ate raw vegetables. We all hung out at Juliano's and bought David "Avocado" Wolfe's *Sunfood Diet*.

Then out of nowhere came this guy Aajonus Vonderplanitz with his prominent yet controversial raw food movement, which consisted of raw milk and dairy products and raw meats, including organs.

People I was close with began blending up bison liver with raw eggs and raw yogurt and drinking it. Yuck.

Then there came the whole vegetarian movement again, and people were going on and on about being vegetarians and the benefits of being vegetarians and writing books about being vegetarians. And then came the vegan movement, but with the vegan movement came a whole cult of personality where people began wearing T-shirts proclaiming meat is murder and protesting.

You would sit down at a restaurant with your friends, and before the waiter could even introduce himself your vegan friends would loudly proclaim, "I am a vegan! What are the vegan options?!" They would lecture anyone who dared order a piece of meat or fish, and when their turn came they would order...eggs.

Some of those exact same people jumped on the whole Paleo movement, which was funny because I remember 20 years earlier when Mark Sisson started the whole Primal movement. It didn't quite catch on at the time, though it seemed to make more sense than just about any fad diet I had heard of.

But this time around you had Paleo/Primal meatheads who were just as bad as the vegans, literally taunting people who didn't eat steak three times a day with raw butter on top of it.

I want to start my own new fad diet right now. It's going to be called the Stop Eating Shit That's Bad for You and Shut the Fuck Up Diet. How about that? How about just eat really healthy food that resonates well with you, and don't talk about it because no one cares. No more seeking your identity through food or standing on a soap box and barking because you are looking for others who are cut from the same cloth to reaffirm your cognitive biases.

You're never going to shame someone into changing. Preaching at people or barking at people and trying to make them feel guilty over what feels right and natural to them is a sure way to reinforce their own cognitive biases, and ultimately makes you look like an idiot.

It's just like with religion. Religion is so beautiful, and I have such respect for all the different religions. There are very few things as cool as driving around the Fairfax district on a Friday and seeing all the Hasidic Jews preparing for Shabbos. The whole family comes together and they eat by candlelight and it's all out of reverence for God. It doesn't get any cooler than that.

Or, if you ever get the chance and you live in a major city, go hang out at the Hare Krishna Temple on a Sunday and just observe what's going on there. I dare you to try and spend more than a few moments without breaking into a huge smile or maybe even joining in the dance with them. They will feed you and they will hug you and they will dance with you. They will dance with complete abandonment, again in reverence towards God. It's so beautiful.

How about watching Easter Sunday Mass with the Pope? You are not alive if you do not feel some sort of wonderment, if you really pay attention.

It is all beautiful.

All religions are beautiful until they try and push themselves on me. Leave me alone. I have come to know God in my own way.

Of all the angry preachers I've seen standing on a street corner, desperately clutching their Bible and screaming at people and threatening them with eternal damnation, I have never seen one single person stop and go, "Oh shit, you're right. Yeah, I should change my ways."

The same goes for diets and food choices. If you see someone walking down the street with a bag of chips and a gallon-sized soda, you won't get them to make healthier choices by screaming at them about diabetes, cancer, obesity and heart disease. Shaming people doesn't work.

BODY WORK

The Magical Benefits of Sauna

I use a sauna almost every day, five out of seven at least. I use two types: a traditional sauna with heated stones and a far-infrared sauna.

I'll often take a decaffeinated green tea extract, sometimes stacking it with turmeric, ginger, black pepper, and cayenne pepper to help with detoxification and to reduce inflammation.

My traditional sauna is great for heat stress, and I love pouring water over the coals to really let my pores open up. It's also a huge help for sore and stiff muscles, especially when paired with cold therapy. I usually keep the sauna around 190 degrees Fahrenheit, spend twenty minutes heat bathing, then hit the cold plunge, repeating as needed typically three or four times. I get some detoxification in the traditional sauna, but if detox is my main goal for the heat session I'll use my far-infrared sauna.

The far-infrared sauna doesn't get as hot as the traditional—it's between 120 and 150 degrees Fahrenheit—but I sweat just as much, if not more, because the far-infrared emitters create energy that heats our bodies from the inside. This is why far-infrared saunas are so much better for detoxification. They literally heat our internal tissues and force perspiration and toxins out of the body.

With my far-infrared unit, I typically do one session of thirty-five minutes between 145-150 degrees Fahrenheit, then hit the cold plunge.

Two or three times a year, I will also incorporate niacin into my sauna ritual for two weeks. I start with 100 mg and gradually work up to 500 milligrams of niacin, which burns fat and detoxifies the body.

I'm extremely careful to add only a little bit of niacin at a time. I once made the mistake of jumping to a full dose of 300 milligrams, and twenty minutes later I was on the floor, writhing in agony and tearing at my skin from the extreme flush and burning sensation. It was a horrific experience, and I almost ended up in the hospital. Please, please use caution if you're going to incorporate niacin.

Again, this is only what works for me. If you want a deeper dive into the health benefits of sauna, check out the information compiled by Dr. Rhonda Patrick and Ben Greenfield. I have links up at khalilrafati.com/sauna.

MIND WORK

Spirituality and Faith

You hear all the time about celebrities getting interrupted while they're trying to have a peaceful meal with their friends and families. I see it happen at the SunLife locations and it makes me cringe. Nobody ever interrupts me—I'm sure as hell not a celebrity—and it's impossible to interrupt me because I always want to chat.

But one time, somebody interrupted me while I was praying, and that bothered me. It wasn't that he wanted to chat—it was what he wanted to chat about.

I pray before every meal. Something created us, and something created the food that nourishes me and keeps me alive. Whatever or whoever that creator is, I'm going to pray and say thank you.

At this particular meal I was incredibly hungry and really wanted to dive in, but I folded my hands and started praying, and some dude came up and grabbed my shoulder and said, "Jesus?"

I look up, confused. "What?"

"Jesus?"

I said, "No, Khalil."

He frowned. "What?"

"I'm Khalil."

"No, are you praying to Jesus?"

"Oh…"

I had a brief moment of anger because first of all, I WAS PRAYING, and second, you never know a stranger's intent when they come up and put their hands on you.

But instead—and also because I was praying, full of peace and gratitude and all of that—I just said, "Yeah, sure."

It was his turn to be confused. How could I be dismissive about who I'm praying to? Because the name and label just don't matter to me.

I pray to God. I don't know what God's name is. I don't even know if God has a name.

If Jesus is truly the son of God, then yes, I pray to Jesus.

If God's name is Yahweh, I pray to Yahweh.

If God's name is Mohammed, I pray to Mohammed.

I don't know. I don't care. I don't want to know. If I had been born in the Australian Outback, or Palestine, or Russia, or Chile, I'd probably have a much different idea about God. And I'm just talking about modern times—put me in a different era and the possibilities are endless.

Whoever or whatever God is, I offer unconditional gratitude and thanks. The name doesn't matter.

"I am the consciousness of God in action. I know it is God working through me, for God works by means of man. 'The Law of the Lord is perfect.' There is a perfect outcome to all my activity. My work is always successful because it is God's work, which is perfect and divine. I have instantly everything I need because I am supplied and governed by God. I always know how to obtain everything I need. 'My God shall supply all your needs according to his riches in glory.' I am full of peace, harmony, and joy. I radiate Divine Love to all mankind. I am now identified with success; I am attracting to myself according to an Immutable Law the circumstances, conditions, ideas, finances, and all things necessary for the unfoldment of my plans. I am Divinely led in all ways. God is prospering me in mind, body, and affairs. I go to sleep every night feeling successful and happy. 'God giveth to his beloved in sleep.' Thank you, Father."

— JOSEPH MURPHY, *Law Of Success*

If you feel the need to change your name to Truth or Sage or something in Sanskrit, that's fine. If you want to start walking around with mala beads and wearing a turban while you do yoga, to each their own. I personally don't think it needs to be that complicated. But whatever you do, keep it consistent.

I'm being a bit of a hypocrite here because my entire house is blanketed with giant crystals, and I have multiple statues of different Hindu deities and a big Buddha fountain in my backyard. But I am not praying to these statues, nor am I trying to adopt another culture's religion. Hinduism is beautiful, but there is so much posing and posturing out here on the West Coast it really weirds me out when I hear people talking about their "guru."

If you would like to simplify things, I can repeat what I wrote in my first book:

> There is only the straight and narrow. It's sort of silly that it took me so long to come to this conclusion. I searched for years, decades in fact. I experimented with massive amounts of hallucinogens and other drugs. I did all the different forms of yoga and breathwork. I bought all the books, dabbled in all of the religions, saw healers and shamans, travelled to vortexes, bought tens of thousands of dollars' worth of crystals and devices I thought would heal me. Lasers, singing bowls, pendants and bracelets. CDs and MP3s on meditation. I traveled all over India for weeks on end. I spent a month in Indonesia going from island to island doing yoga and chanting. I've been hugged by so-called living Saints and took the Transcendental Meditation course.
>
> In the end, there is only the straight and narrow. The only thing I ever needed

to know was written in the Bible, and that is to love God before all else and to love my neighbor as I love myself. That's it, that's the whole truth. There's nothing more I ever need to know about spirituality or God.

There is only one judge of who I am and what I am and that is my Creator. I believe all of us will be quite shocked when we take our final breath and find our convictions shattered to pieces by the real unifying truth of our timeless existence. But for now, here on this earth, I am glad to finally understand that there is only the straight and narrow—the path of love, truth, compassion, kindness and hard work. Each day I fall short of the mark, but each morning when I am blessed with another try I make a pact with myself to do my best.

It makes me really sad to think how close I came to missing it all. I turned my life into such a mess that I couldn't even kill myself correctly. And in the midst of all of that madness, all of that grace and all of the beautiful recovery that has taken place in the last twelve years, I forgot to die.

Forward

It's simple.

Sobriety, success, being in great shape. Fill in the blank for whatever you're missing in your life.

It is so practical and simple but the mind and the ego want to make it complicated, procrastinate, give credit to luck, or dismiss it altogether and go on suffering.

I am not brave or smart or stronger than most.

I am not wise or fearless or any of the things people have credited me with over the last few years because of the things I now have on the outside.

I am quite naïve and unskilled. But one quality that I do possess is the quality of still remaining a child on the inside. I still dream and imagine and visualize and believe.

For the most part I look for the good in things and for the good in people and I am insanely optimistic, even in my darkest times.

Don't get me wrong—I can sink into a motherfucker of a depression. But there is always some part of me that's tapping me on the shoulder saying, "No, no, no, you're going to get through this and there are great things coming your way!"

Just like a child I can fall flat on my face. I can hit the ground hard with a loud smacking sound and even though it hurts I will set aside that pain and quickly jump back up on my feet and continue trudging forward.

Sooner or later the pain wears off. Sooner or later the hard fall becomes a distant memory. But more importantly, the progress continues. The tiny little incremental steps towards each goal.

I just keep moving forward.

My head catches fire every morning when I wake up and it is full of fear and doubt and insecurity, but I get out of bed, pound some espresso and start moving. I just keep moving forward and I don't stop.

I do not possess any great skills or talents. Just the ability to get up and keep moving forward.

Maybe on the outside it looks like fearlessness, but it is quite the contrary.

I am frightened.

I am scared as hell.

I am riddled with fear a lot of the time, but my greatest fear is not living the life that I am capable of living.

My greatest fear is laying on my deathbed someday in a fetal position, agonizing over what I could have done or should have done or might have done. That fear wakes me up in the middle of the night and I toss and turn and wrestle with my existential angst.

That fear will produce an overwhelming sense of impending doom at times for no apparent reason. That fear will sometimes envelop me in a fatalistic blanket of hopelessness.

But I just get up and keep moving.

I say, "Good morning" to my fear.

I acknowledge its presence. I am well aware of the strength and power of my fear and what it could do to me, where it could take me.

But I am also acutely aware of the power of my creator, my God, my angels, whatever or whoever is watching over me and has given me this life. The power of my creator is infinitely stronger than any fear or challenge that comes my way.

I work hard at keeping close to my creator. I have a constant dialogue, as if this best friend is walking by my side at all times and holding my hand when I am scared.

I can say in any moment, "God, please be with me now. God, can you please hold my hand. God, please walk me through this difficult moment. Please let me know that you are here with me now."

Before each meal I give thanks and praise. Each time I look at a beautiful sunrise or sunset I give thanks and praise. With each victory I say, "Thank you God, thank you thank you thank you!"

ABUNDANCE

Your goals don't care how you feel.

Money Absolutely Can Buy You Happiness...

The saying that money can't buy you happiness is a lie.

I know what it's like to do hard manual labor. I know what it's like to be poor. I got my first job when I was twelve, and I did whatever menial tasks someone would pay me to do until I was thirty-six. I was grateful for the work. It was no one's fault but mine that I was basically unemployable.

I know what it's like to be among the 78% of workers in this country living paycheck to paycheck[1]. To be in massive credit card debt that increases every day because of astronomical interest rates. To make fear-based decisions about money and live in a mindset of scarcity. To be part of the 29% of American households with less than $1,000 in savings[2].

To fight all the time with my girlfriend over which bills we can pay and which ones we can't. To take her out for a nice dinner a few times a year, and scour the menu for the cheapest items.

---

1 https://www.cnbc.com/2019/01/09/shutdown-highlights-that-4-in-5-us-workers-live-paycheck-to-paycheck.html

2 https://www.magnifymoney.com/blog/news/average-american-savings/

It is awful. It is a terrible existence. I felt trapped. I felt like I had no options.

And what happened when I went from working my ass off and doing what I had to do for twenty thousand dollars a year, to working my ass off for one hundred thousand dollars a year, doing what I wanted to do?

When I went from not being able to open a checking account because of my debt to having fifty grand in savings?

I was exponentially happier.

Money can make the difference between doing what you **have** to do and doing what you **want** to do.

It creates options.

And it's not about the option to add things. It's the option to eliminate them.

Eliminate stress. When I stopped worrying about when my paycheck would clear so I could pay overdue bills, my stress plummeted. I could breathe again.

Eliminate fear. The fear that if my mother got sick, I wouldn't be able to care for her. When I knew I could afford to help her, that fear went away.

Eliminate shame. The shame that I couldn't provide my girlfriend with a better life. When we could pay the bills and go out to eat without worrying about the bill, our relationship got better because we weren't fighting about money all the time.

It felt amazing. I slept better. I was able to be present and problem-solve creatively instead of worrying about the future, making fear-based decisions about how to keep the water and electricity on.

Having that money absolutely made me happier.

. . .To a Certain Extent

But when I went from making one hundred grand a year to three hundred grand, I didn't get three times happier. I didn't feel three times safer and lose three times more stress. My lifestyle and level of comfort and security were already where I wanted them to be.

Once I hit a certain level of income and savings, and knew I could stay there, my happiness was all about mindset. My ability to coexist in this world with my fellow human beings and try my best to be the person that God intended me to be. And these were abilities I already had, I just wasn't able to express or engage with them until I was financially stable. I did not feel like I had the choice to be happy. Once I had enough money, that all changed.

Enough—that is a vital point to make. If your goal is to be rich, what does that mean? A million dollars? Ten million? For me, being rich meant not having to worry about paying bills. Anything beyond that is icing on the cake.

And I will make more money than I have now. Not because that's the goal—it's just a result of doing what I love to do. But I will never be happier than I am now because of money.

In this moment, there is no amount of money that's going to make me happier.

Dreams do come true!

Kneeling down in my new home in a moment of gratitude. Looking at this incredibly inspiring image of Kelly Slater and John John Florence that Todd Glaser captured on film. My self-doubting, hypercritical mind always told me I'd never be able to afford a home. It was right as long as I believed it.

Then one day someone told me that God loved me and wanted me to have abundance and prosperity. His name was Charles Quint. He kept repeating it over and over to me every time we spoke. After about 6 months I started to believe him. Thirty-three years of negative programming began to form cracks.

Then Cindy Landon gifted me the DVD of *The Secret* which I watched about 1,000 times.

Then a stranger told me about Napoleon Hill's book *Think and Grow Rich*.

Then, then, then…

It didn't happen overnight. It took fifteen years and a lot of hard work. But thank God for the people who came into my life and helped along the way. Thank God I bottomed out so hard with drugs and alcohol and got into so much pain that I became teachable!

Thank God for my sobriety!

So now I'm returning the favor and passing on the wisdom to you.

God loves you and wants you to be happy.

God wants you to have abundance and prosperity!

Don't waste your time burning incense and putting on fancy oils.

Just get on your knees and ask God for help and get to work.

From now on, walk forward confidently towards your dreams as if you have an armed guard walking beside you!

First Class State of Mind

I'll never forget the first time I flew first class. It was 2010, and Hayley and I were together at the time, flying to Hawaii to spend the holidays with our business partner Rick. We never would have booked that flight at all, let alone in first class, if Rick hadn't paid for all of it.

When I looked at the tickets and realized he'd put us in first class I thought, "That is so dumb. Why would you ever spend fifteen hundred dollars on a ticket when you could spend six hundred?"

It made zero sense. Of course, at that time my only experience with flying had been putting a six-hundred dollar ticket on my credit card and spending a thousand dollars to pay it off because of interest fees.

I got even more confused at the airport when the person at the desk fired up the microphone to board us and said, "We will now begin boarding our first class and Medallion members."

I thought, "What is going on here? Isn't first class in the front of the plane? Why would they seat us first? These people are stupid."

But I lined up with the other people in first class anyway, and that's when the whole thing started to make sense. I looked at the passengers in that line and they all had this **thing** about them. Their shoulders were back. Their heads were high. They were smiling. Some were holding hands. When they moved forward they moved with confidence.

I whispered, "Ohhhh."

Hayley heard me and looked over. "What?"

"First class is a state of mind."

She said, "What do you mean?"

"I don't think these people are any smarter or any better or any luckier than other people. I think these people just think they're smarter and better and luckier, and maybe they don't even consciously think it. But I looked at every one of them, and they absolutely, positively had a look on their face like they deserved to be in first class."

We strolled with that group onto the plane and didn't have to wait in the jetway, which is always either freezing cold or broiling hot. We didn't have to rush to find a spot to cram our carry-on bags. We eased into our wide seats, which could extend all the way flat into a bed, and were immediately offered champagne.

I thought, *Champagne? What the hell? What are these people celebrating?*

Then it hit me again.

Oh, right. They're celebrating being in first class. They made it.

We had free access to all of the entertainment options. The flight attendant offered us nice, big headphones, not the nasty little buds that fall out of your ears. I looked around at everyone toasting each other and understood why people pay three times as much to upgrade to first class. It made them feel three times more special. The plane takes off and lands at the exact same place, but the trip is entirely different.

This was reinforced even more when the coach passengers boarded. I got some looks of curiosity, resentment, envy, and even a few nods of congratulations as if I'd done something significant. It was another reason to seat us first. Everybody else has to file past while we're on display and the airline whispers to them, "You too can have all of this for just three times the price."

But here's the craziest part: When the plane took off, I started to put my seat back, and it kept going...and going...and going until it was all the way flat. It was a bed! I slept like a baby with a giant smile on my face, and the experience of travel was changed forever.

When I woke up on the descent to Hawaii I leaned over to Hayley and said, "I'm going to keep working my ass off until we can always fly first class without ever worrying about the price."

She said, "Good for you."

I took it all in. It was an amazing gift from my friend to fly first class, and I knew it would feel even better once I was able to pay for it myself. It became a powerful motivator for me. Not just the bigger seats, better movies and better food—it really had nothing to do with flying.

I had acquired the first class state of mind. I was prepared to do whatever it took to earn that lifestyle.

Here I am ten years later, and I gotta tell you, two of the greatest things about making money that I get to experience are never again having to be rudely woken by an alarm clock and the joy of flying first class whenever I want.

We are so lucky to be alive and living in this moment!

If we look for the good we will find it. It works the other way, too. Let us look for the good. Let us praise God!

Never in the history of the world has quality of life been better. Never in the history of the world have people lived longer.

If you are reading this, chances are you have a roof over your head and you will not go hungry today.

If you are reading this, chances are you have clean water.

If you are reading this, chances are you are not living in a war zone.

If you are reading this, you are luckier and more comfortable than 99% of the people who have existed on this planet.

Today is an incredible day regardless of your political views.

Today is a magical day because we are alive, so let's love each other.

And if you are still hell-bent on believing that the world is falling apart and you want to change it, then go home and love your children. Give them a hug and tell them you love them. Or your girlfriend or your best friend or your neighbor.

Go love somebody. Go be kind to somebody.

Smile at people when you walk past them regardless of their demeanor or disposition.

Pick up trash when you see it; return your shopping cart to the front of the store, even if it's raining.

Tip your server 20% even if it's the worst service you've ever had.

We are all in this together!

We might as well love one another and be kind to one another and make this existence as enjoyable as possible through acts of kindness and love.

It is Incredibly Expensive to be Poor

Once we started making some money at SunLife Organics, we started getting unbelievable offers from credit card companies. They were unbelievable because I wasn't far removed from missing credit card payments and not being able to get a checking account, and now American Express wanted to give me a card with seventy thousand travel miles on it.

The basic message was, "We want people like you to be seen using our card."

I was blown away. After a few offers like that I had another first class "Aha" moment. I realized that having money and creating wealth is just a game. The more money I made, the more free stuff I got. And not useless trinkets or junk, I'm talking free travel miles, clothes, hotel rooms and services, meals. Entire vacations.

It's all a game, and the game is of course rigged in favor of the wealthy. It is incredibly cheap to be rich, and it is tragically expensive to be poor.

When I was broke I had a variable interest rate on my credit card that went as high as 29.9%. That's insane. That's how I wound up paying $1,000 for a $600 ticket, and the credit card companies loved me for it. It wasn't American Express, but the message was similar: "We want people like you to stay broke using our card."

I was an indentured servant to them.

Compounding interest...You are either the victim of it or the grateful recipient. In other words, you're either making a bunch of money from it via your investments, or you're getting fucked because of your credit card debt and/or loans.

And now that I have enough money to afford everything I could want and need, I'm rewarded by getting a bunch of stuff for free. All of my airline tickets are free because of my credit card points. I even use credit card points to pay off my credit card bills sometimes. Because I'm a private banker I don't get charged any of the fees that typically apply.

I don't have overdraft charges.

I don't have ATM charges anywhere in the world.

I don't get charged to send or receive wire transfers.

And the craziest part is now that I have money and my credit score is so good, I get ridiculously low rates if I want to borrow money. But the people who don't have money and desperately need to borrow it have to pay insanely high rates because their scores aren't as good.

I didn't fully realize it until I'd experienced both ends of the spectrum, but here's the harsh truth: **We are domesticated animals bred for debt and taxation.**

If you are stuck in that insidious cycle, rotating from the trough to the slaughterhouse and back again beneath the weight of crushing debt, shuffling your way toward failure and regret...

THE POWER OF CHANGE CAN SET YOU FREE

Detachment is not that you own nothing.

Detachment is that nothing owns you.

I love what I do. I love serving people and making a difference in their lives and in the communities we're lucky enough to belong to. I love bringing value to my employees and customers. I love writing books that help people around the world.

The best way to continue serving and bringing value, to make a bigger difference and reach more communities, is to stay in business and grow.

That's what keeps me going. That's what makes me happy.

Entrepreneurship: The ability to run through walls.

Addicted to Happiness

I'm an addict, and I am addicted to feeling amazing. I'm addicted to happiness.

Making people smile feels amazing to me. I do things that make other people happy, which makes me happy.

My happiness goes everywhere with me.

My peace of mind is always inside me.

My love collects no dust.

The #1 Life Improvement Biohack

I'm lucky enough to have direct access to some of the most brilliant health, wellness, and nutrition minds of this era.

Of all the different tools I've acquired, and all the so-called biohacks I've learned and utilized, and all the different recipes and ingredients I use and love—and some of them are absolutely life changing—I truly believe that kindness is the number-one most undervalued and underused tool that we have access to.

Just being kind.

Will being kind guarantee you a flat stomach, your dream home, and plenty of cash for traveling the world?

No...but it won't prevent any of that either.

And it's free.

You don't have to be a cold-blooded cutthroat sociopath to be successful.

It's easy and lazy to vilify successful people as manipulative and conniving because it lets us off the hook.

I guess I'll never be that successful because I'm not an asshole.

I know a ton of highly successful people, and the majority of them are kind and loving human beings.

They're just good people.

Some of the most patient, compassionate customers who come into SunLife happen to be worth millions of dollars because of businesses they built through hard work, sacrifice, and yes, kindness.

Do I know rich assholes?

Of course.

Do I know broke assholes?

Absolutely.

But success isn't a factor in their behavior. The broke assholes won't suddenly gain compassion along with a few commas in their bank account, and the rich ones won't become kind should they lose everything.

Kindness relies on being kind, and nothing else.

Being kind makes life better, but it doesn't protect you from life.

I saw this firsthand with my mother, who I am eternally grateful to for passing her kindness along to me, despite some very determined attempts on my part to stray from it.

My mother was kind to everyone. Her ability to make people feel special borders on a super power. On a trip back home years ago I took her around on her errands, and everywhere we went people practically cheered when she walked in.

The construction workers on her street—complete strangers when the project started—got homemade snacks and cookies from her every day.

They all knew and loved her because of her kindness and compassion toward everyone.

But life was not kind to her.

During World War II my grandmother was forced to give my mother up as a child in order to survive. My mother's living conditions after that led to malnutrition and a lifetime of health problems. Her marriage to my father was a living hell of abuse, and after their divorce she struggled to pay her bills.

On top of it all, she had to deal with me...

Still, through it all, she chose kindness.

Making money and saving money and investing money and eating the right things and exercising and intermittent fasting and saunas and everything else I talk about in this book—they can all make life better.

They can make life amazing.

But it all means nothing if you're going to be a dick.

Don't be a dick.

The single most common regret of the dying is wishing they had the courage to live a life true to themselves and not the life expected of them by others.

That's the whole secret of life. It sounds so simple and cliché but to really, truly love yourself and accept yourself, that is the key to happiness and success.

Mindset

Stop.

Push pause.

Take a deep breath.

What are you grateful for?

Make a list. Put pen to paper.

Right down twenty things you're grateful for.

Start with clean water and a roof over your head.

Millions of people don't have either.

Once you're done, make a one-year, a three-year and a five-year plan of who and where you will be.

Again, put pen to paper. Be as detailed as possible.

Then begin walking towards your goals and don't give up until you've acquired each and every one.

This is not a dress rehearsal. And don't allow yourself to believe it's too late.

I didn't get sober until I was 33.

I didn't start SunLife until I was 41.

I didn't write my first book until I was 46.

Age is a state of mind.

Just like everything else.

"Monday doesn't suck. The weather doesn't suck. Your job doesn't suck. Your negative mindset sucks. Your lack of self-worth and self love sucks."

—JIM CARREY

Choose Kindness

I was treating two wonderful friends to brunch at a seaside restaurant, and I was feeling really good. I was proud that I could take them to this place and provide them with an amazing meal in the sunshine and fresh air while we talked and laughed together.

I left the table to get an omelet and I was the only person in line, which made the day even better. The chef manning the omelet station seemed really flustered, tossing pans and utensils around. He looked at me and nodded, but with panic on his face. Then he left.

He was obviously off to a rough start. I wasn't sure if he had to use the bathroom, or wasn't feeling well...but regardless I just kept waiting.

Another customer stepped next to me and I glanced over to say good morning, and I couldn't help noticing what he was wearing.

Fendi pants, a blouse-like shirt with a collar that turned into a scarf, and what looked like a very expensive hat.

His outfit alone was well into the thousands—forget about his watch and jewelry.

He was obviously wealthy and enjoyed the look and feel of expensive clothes.

He was also furious.

A woman in equally expensive attire came up next to him, and he said, "I don't know what's going on. This is taking forever. Do you want me to order you an omelet?"

She seemed indifferent about it, but said, "Yeah, I'll take one."

I just stood there, waiting.

Then one of the table bussers came up with a stack of plates and dropped them off at the omelet station.

Mr. Fancy Pants started snapping his fingers.

"Excuse me! Excuse me!"

The busser didn't hear him, or didn't think he was the target of the snapping, so he didn't turn around.

Mr. Fancy Pants raised his voice.

"Hey, dude, do you work here? Am I supposed to make this omelet myself?"

I was horrified.

My blood surged.

I wanted to grab his snapping fingers and snap them in half.

I was on the brink of unleashing hell upon this asshole and showing him what it felt like to be humiliated and berated.

But I caught myself.

If I bite this guy's head off, I'm no different than him.

I become the asshole.

Maybe he's dealing with something overwhelming.

Maybe he has low blood sugar and can't handle it.

It didn't really matter.

There's never an excuse to treat someone the way he was treating the restaurant employee, and I was about to treat Mr. Fancy Pants the same exact way.

Inexcusable.

So I took a deep breath and bit my tongue.

After a few more minutes a manager came over, and Mr. Fancy Pants turned on him.

The manager handled it well—unfortunately this sort of entitled behavior isn't uncommon in private Malibu clubs—and he apologized and tried to get the omelet station going himself.

Mr. Fancy Pants said, "Yeah, good. I want bacon. I want onions..."

And I couldn't take it any longer.

I looked at Mr. Fancy Pants and in a very calm, reasonable tone said, "You do realize that I was here before you."

"Yeah, well, I've been trying to get an omelet for forty-five minutes now."

Not, "Oh, I'm so sorry, I didn't realize."

Not, "Yes, I know, and thank you for your understanding."

My temper flared again.

I wanted so badly to unload.

Or if not unload, at least grab the scarf at the top of his blouse and gently begin to tighten the material while staring deeply and maniacally into his eyes.

I had to turn away and reach within to calm myself again.

I took another deep breath and said, "Look, if it means that much to you, go right ahead."

Shockingly he accepted and began rattling off his order.

At that point, all I could do was laugh.

And the whole time the restaurant staff worked in a frenzy to get this guy his omelet, I struggled to leave it at that.

I swung wildly between fury and compassion.

Put this asshole in his place, now!

You'd be no better than him.

He has it coming! He's being a dick!

Maybe he's going through some shit right now that you can't begin to comprehend. Maybe his mother is sick. Maybe he's on the verge of a divorce...

Finally he got his omelet and walked away.

I slowly began to settle down. A new omelet guy showed up and made mine, and while he worked I realized what I needed to do.

I found the manager, the one who had been yelled at while he tried to figure out the omelet station.

He saw me coming and looked like he was preparing himself for another round of Mr. Fancy Pants treatment.

Before he could get a word out I said, "I am so sorry."

He was stunned. "You're sorry? For what? I was going to apologize to you because you had to wait for your omelet."

I said, "No, no, I don't mind waiting at all. I am so sorry that you had to deal with such a fucking asshole."

The look on his face—it was pure appreciation for being seen and acknowledged.

He said, "Honestly, man, it's not the first time."

I nodded. "I know. And that's the worst part. I'm in the food service industry too, and sometimes I have to deal with similar things. But I try to go out of my way and serve people to the best of my ability. We never really know what they're going through that makes them treat other people so harshly."

He said, "Wow, man. I really want to thank you for stopping and checking in."

I said, "Yeah, man. I just want to thank you for helping out and again, apologize for what you had to go through."

"Thank you so much."

And we had our little bromance moment, and it was wonderful.

Because I have not always chosen kindness.

I've been Mr. Fancy Pants.

Recalling those moments of selfish entitlement, when I was too caught up in whatever I was going through to realize how cruel I was being to another human being, makes me sick to my stomach.

I went back to the table and joined my friends. We sat in the sun and ate and talked and basked in life, and I silently prayed for the strength to always choose kindness over everything else.

My pride, my ego, my sense of justice, my expectations…

Kindness and love over everything.

If we can evolve to that level and always try our best to be kind, everything else will fall into place.

Give Relentlessly, Generously, and Unconditionally

Give.

Giving relentlessly, generously, and unconditionally brings me endless joy. I don't like talking about this part of my life because it may come off as bragging. I'm definitely a show-off, but not when it comes to this. I never talk about this part of my life.

Not only is bragging about generosity pathetic and gross, it destroys the whole purpose of giving. As soon as you seek attention for your generosity, it's tainted.

It's the same as placing conditions, judgement and expectations on a gift or act of kindness. If I give twenty bucks to a homeless person, I won't say, "Now, don't you go spending this on drugs. What you should really do is put yourself on a ketogenic diet and get some healthy fats to your brain..."

No. It's a gift, and it's none of my business what they do with the money. In fact, if they take the money and get high, good for them. For all I know, they could be minutes away from jumping into oncoming traffic because they are so suicidally depressed. There were times in my life when I absolutely, positively needed to get high because I was in such a dark place with no hope. So I thank God for the strangers who handed me money when I was panhandling.

Take it, use it to make yourself happy, whatever that means.

In 2005, my sponsor Robbie tried teaching me about tithing. He was really harping on me about it, telling me I had to tithe, you gotta tithe, tithing is essential. He was all wound up about it.

I asked him, "What the hell is tithing?"

Turns out, it's giving money to a church or organization and the idea comes from the Bible, where it tells us to take ten percent of annual earnings and give to those who are less fortunate. When they pass the basket or bowl around and people put money in, that's tithing.

Of course, I didn't have an annual income, so Robbie just told me it was ten percent of whatever I had. If I had ten dollars, I should give one. If I had a hundred, I should give ten. We were sitting in a twelve-step meeting and they started passing the basket around, and he told me it was time to tithe.

I said, "Dude, I'm broke and homeless. The only reason I'm not living under a bridge is because you let me crash at your place."

"It doesn't matter," he said. "You have money in your pocket. Put the money in."

I looked around and saw people putting single dollar bills in. I shook my head and pulled out one of my precious dollars.

Robbie said, "I paid you one hundred bucks to wash my car. Put two in the basket."

"Two!?"

"Yes, just to show God how much faith you have in him that he's going to take care of you."

I couldn't believe it. The bowl came to me and I clutched my two dollars above it, unable to fathom why I was throwing cash away. But I put the two dollars in the bowl and passed it along, and you know what?

It felt amazing.

Maybe it was because I was doing right by Robbie; maybe it was because I was helping to support the twelve-step meeting that was helping so many others; maybe it was because this little gesture showed God I had faith.

Whatever it was, those private moments of putting money I thought I couldn't afford to lose into the bowl and passing it along made me feel great.

Of course, typical me, I figured if two bucks felt that good, five bucks would be euphoric. So I waited for a time when I knew other people were watching and I tossed a five in, just to show off.

It felt terrible.

I had sullied the moment, turned it selfish and narcissistic. Instead of a private moment between me and God, it became a "look at me" opportunity. And I wasn't doing it to make other people happy. I was doing it to come off like some kind of martyr or saint. Yuck.

After a few more experiences like that I never did it again.

Give without conditions or expectations. You will be amazed by how good it makes you feel.

God wants you to be rich and have everything you want.

It's true.

When I was newly sober and broke and sleeping on my friend's floor because I couldn't afford a bed or apartment I used to call this guy that lived in the valley named Charles.

Every day I had troubles and overwhelming fears and anxieties. I used to call him all the time and try to explain my troubles to him and try to explain my fears. Every single time I would do this he would listen patiently and then he would say the same thing over and over. "Khalil, God wants you to be rich."

It was frustrating because first and foremost, he wasn't rich at all! In fact I think he was pretty broke.

Secondly he was a black dude from the south that had a good shot at playing professional football, but he destroyed his career because of his drinking and drug use.

I couldn't help but think, "Why didn't God want him to be rich? Why didn't God want him to play pro ball?"

I missed the fact that God did, but Charles had other plans.

God had blessed Charles with these amazing talents, but instead of accepting them and utilizing them and living up to his fullest potential, Charles decided to drink instead. As I got to know him better and he told me more and more stories, it turns out he had second chance after second chance, but continued to drink and throw away his football career.

Charles told me so many times that God wanted me to be rich that I guess one day I just started to believe him. I started to believe that God wanted me to be rich and the moment I did my life really began to change. I started looking for proof that God wanted me to be rich, and all the proof I ever needed was right in front of my face!

I don't know what happened to Charles. I heard he went back to school and finally finished college and earned a degree in psychology with plans to practice as a therapist.

Well here I am 14 years later and I am rich! I became rich because I managed to shift out of the poverty mentality that had been instilled deep within my being. I went from a scarcity mentality to one of abundance. I had a paradigm shift.

Give What Cannot be Bought

I'm nervous about this. Telling this story can easily come off as bragging. I promise you it is not. I want to illustrate how powerful giving can be, and not just when it comes to money.

There is a man I see every day who works at multiple businesses around one of the Sun-Life locations, no matter what time of day it is. During the day he works at one spot, and in the evening he works at a restaurant a few doors down. His work ethic is unbelievable.

We chatted a few times, somewhat awkwardly because of a language barrier, talking about work and families. I found out he has a wife and three daughters, which explained why he works so hard. Despite the lack of a translator we got along very well and made each other laugh.

One day he came into SunLife with his youngest daughter, who looked about seven or eight, and they were both grinning ear-to-ear. The girl was excited to try one of our smoothies and her father was brimming with pride about being able to provide her with such a treat. My heart swelled at the sight of them.

I greeted them like old friends, telling the father, "It's so good to see you! Welcome!"

I hugged him and said whatever they wanted, it was on the house. The girl looked from me to her father and back. I was showing her father respect and she picked up on it. Her smile grew even more.

Giving the gift of respect cost me nothing, but it was more valuable than anything on our menu by far. Seeing how good it made that girl and her father feel put me over the moon.

After that, I went out of my way to say hello to the father when I was at that location. On hot days I'd carry a juice into the back of the sweltering building and hand it to him, say hello, and be on my way. I never wanted him to feel like I felt sorry for him. I considered him my friend, and that's what I would do for a friend.

A few months after the father and daughter came into the shop I hit a streak of really great luck. I went on a trip with one of my best friends as his good luck charm in a high-stakes poker tournament. I risked a pretty big chunk of cash betting that he would win, and he ended up doing just that. But he didn't just win—he won big.

When I got back home I saw the father working, grinding as hard as ever, and it hit me: Why not break him off a piece of the winnings? I hesitated, fearful about offending him; I didn't want him to think I saw him as some charity case. But I finally said screw it.

I ran to the bank and withdrew a chunk of cash. Then I found the father again and asked him to follow me out back. We stood there looking at each other for a moment, then I handed him the wad of money.

Understandably, he freaked out.

"No, no, no!" he said. "What are you doing? What are you doing?"

He had no idea what was going on and it was made worse by the fact that English was his second language, and I sure as hell didn't speak Spanish.

I tried to calm him down. "Hey, man, listen, take the money. I won it. Okay? Gambling. I was gambling. God blessed me. I have to share it."

He understood that part and his eyes welled with tears. He said, "I can't take this. I can't take this."

"I know. It's not for you. It's for your daughters."

His eyes welled up even more, then I started crying, then I laughed because I was crying, and he started laughing with me. It was wonderful. One of the best moments of my life. And I have to be honest with you, and maybe it's not appropriate to say this, but I felt high as I got back into my car. I was high AF, as the kids like to say.

And that feeling has stayed with me. It's with me now, as I write this. This has nothing to do with being a good guy, or being virtuous. This shit is common sense. When you're winning, why not share? And it doesn't have to be winning at gambling, it can just be winning at life. If we're winning at life, it's common sense that we should share with those less fortunate than us.

I'm sure you can see why I'm hesitant to share this story. Until now it was between me and my creator, as it should be. The last thing I want to do is taint that experience by bringing selfish attention to it.

But I do want to illustrate the power of seeking out opportunities to acknowledge and appreciate what someone else is going through. We're all in this together, and we all need a gift now and then. That man deserved respect, and he deserved a break. I hope that money bought him and his family a little bit of happiness.

For me, it's one of the best investments I've ever made.

Build a Lifestyle that Benefits You and Others

I've never wanted an ordinary life. A lot of what I do reminds me of when I was just a boy and I had this crazy idea to build a bike ramp in my friend's backyard.

I planned it all out. We would fly down the hill, hit the ramp, and jump over this creek that ran through the property.

Everybody thought I was crazy. They said there was no way it would work. But they followed me over to the house, and for a while they watched me piling dirt and rocks and boards up into a ramp. Then, even though they kept telling me it was crazy and would never work, they joined in and helped.

I think they helped for two reasons: They wanted to believe it could be done, and they wanted to see me fail. And it wasn't one or the other. I think everybody there wanted it to work just as much as they wanted to see me crash.

When we were all satisfied with the construction job I took my little yellow Schwinn bike to the top of the hill and stared down at the pile of dirt we'd made. I tried to look cool, though I was scared to death. I couldn't breathe. It felt like the house and trees and yard were closing in around me.

But there was no going back. Even as a kid, once I decided I was going to do something there was no stopping me.

I pushed off and pedaled as hard as I could down that hill. I hit the ramp, felt the impact through the pedals and handlebars, and I flew over that creek. Everyone lost their minds, yelling and screaming and cheering. I did it a few more times without dying, and at that point the other kids finally accepted the fact that it was possible.

It sure as hell wasn't safe, and I wouldn't call it smart. But it was possible.

That is my compass. My mindset. Tell me something is insane, impossible, outrageous, extraordinary, and it gets moved to the top of my to-do list. My only real skill is that I don't give up, and while I started out with stupid stunts like the ramp, and as I grew older I unfortunately applied that unstoppable drive to drugs and partying.

When I was on drugs my sole focus was myself and getting high. My next fix. That was it. I was just a selfish junkie.

When I was in recovery and finally getting sober, I clamped onto the need to stay clean like a pit bull. I grabbed on with my teeth and wouldn't let go.

Thankfully, I came out of recovery with my relentless mindset intact. But I had gained the gift of wanting to apply it to something other than myself. I wanted it to benefit others for once. The opportunity to do so hit me like a truck when my mother got cancer eight months into my sobriety.

I thought I had been working hard for those eight months, but I was wrong. When my mom got cancer, I realized I had no means to help her. She was still working and had some money and insurance, but that wouldn't cover everything, and I didn't have any money to put toward her medical bills. I wasn't there to take her to doctor appointments. I couldn't even afford to fly back to Ohio to visit her. That night I went back to the guest house I was staying in and imagined her suffering alone for the next year, three years, five years, slowly dying with no one there to take care of her. I sobbed for hours and cried myself to sleep that night.

That experience scared the shit out of me. I discovered a new gear of intensity, working three or four jobs at a time. I was a man possessed. I saved everything and took huge financial risks because of the massive potential upside.

As soon as my savings account hit the goal I'd set I jumped on a plane with Hayley and flew to Ohio. After seeing how my mom was doing and how she was living, which was in Kenwood Gardens, basically a housing project, the first thing I did was call a realtor. My mom was going to beat the cancer, and I wanted to make sure she was as comfortable as possible in her own home while she did it.

The realtor had three houses on his list, and my mom hated the first two, which was hilarious considering where she was living. As we walked up to the third house she commented about how much she liked the tree in the front yard, and once we got inside she admired the hardwood floors.

I turned to the realtor. "We'll take it."

"Um, don't you want to negotiate?"

"No, I don't. I don't care. I'm not looking to make money on this. I just want my mom to be safe and live in a beautiful house on this beautiful street. That's it."

I set up an annuity to make sure she had enough money every month to live comfortably, and eventually I got her to retire so she could focus on taking care of herself.

The entire time, all I wanted was to make sure she was okay. That she got whatever she needed. That she felt loved and cared for and special. And I had no idea how great doing that would make me feel.

My mom and I never had a good relationship, but once I knew my mom was set for the rest of her life, a huge burden lifted from me. Working my ass off to make life better for her was exponentially more rewarding than doing it to buy myself a new car, watch, whatever stupid shiny thing that doesn't really matter. By moving the focus off of myself, the work didn't even feel like work anymore. It was a cause. A mission.

As I write this, my mother is in an assisted living home. We talk almost every day, and she always mentions how incredibly comfortable and happy she is. The caretakers send me photos of her baking cookies, enjoying her scandalous cheesecake dessert, and participating in group exercises.

It fills me with incredible joy knowing I could do that for her. It is the single most important accomplishment of my life and will ever remain so.

Earn Your Rocking Chair

Someone once said to me, "Imagine yourself at eighty-seven years old, sitting in a rocking chair."

We were in Malibu, looking at the ocean.

He said, "Maybe you're here. Or maybe you're in Bali, or—"

I cut him off and said, "How about both?"

He smiled. "Okay, how about both? Now imagine you're sitting in that rocking chair with a big smile on your face. What are the things you've accomplished that would put that smile on your face?"

I thought about it for about ten seconds. "I've already done it. I've already accomplished those things."

Truly Giving Back

I was talking with a young man attending Stanford, which can cost seventy thousand dollars per year at the time of this writing. It's probably more now.

I asked him, "Dude, what are you gonna do when you get out with that mountain of debt?"

"Oh, my dad worked his butt off. He wasn't able to go to college, so he worked like crazy and saved up his money, and my parents are able to pay for my schooling. I won't have any debt."

I was floored. When I was young I had a dream to be a rock star or a movie star. I think a lot of us do. But screw that. I want to be that kid's dad.

He's a true rock star. He's my hero. He did what he had to do to give his child a world-class education, and as I write this that child is attending classes taught by Peter Thiel and Condoleezza Rice.

I hope that one day, that kid can go to his parents and say, "You've done what you had to do my entire life. I am happy. I am successful. Now go do what you **want** to do. It's on me."

In 2018 I was lucky enough to have dinner with Condoleezza Rice. I was blessed with the incredible opportunity to go with my friend Kelly to the Ryder Cup. The Ryder Cup is a golf event, and it includes a charity tournament filled with celebrities. Kelly was an invited guest and I was his plus one.

We were eating dinner at Ralph Lauren's private restaurant in Paris—I didn't even know Ralph Lauren had a restaurant, but he does—sitting at a table with Condoleezza Rice, Kurt Russell, Greg Kinnear, Samuel L. Jackson and one of the Jonas brothers. I don't know which one.

The meal lasted for a few hours, and every now and then I would look at Kelly to my right, then around the table at everyone else, and I'd get overwhelmed with how surreal it all was.

They were all debating current events, and I just sat there with my ego urging me to say something, to contribute, but I resisted and found myself perfectly content being the dumbest person in the room and keeping my mouth shut, which is how you learn. And I learned a ton.

I mean, I learned so much from Condoleezza Rice in just a few hours—imagine what that young man taking her class at Stanford will learn. What an amazing gift.

While we were at the Ryder Cup I reached out to a man I'd met in Paris a few months earlier, Milutin Gatsby, a good friend and the Global Fundraising Chairman for The Foundation for AIDS Research, or amfAR.

When I told him I was in Paris, he said, "My brother, you should come to my charity event in Monaco!"

I said, "Oh, sure. Can I bring my friend Kelly?"

"Of course, I will make the arrangements. Is Kelly a man or a woman?"

"He's a guy, Kelly Slater. He's the surfer guy."

Milutin said, "Oh, my God, yes, please invite him. Look, this charity event is for cleaning up the oceans. It's an auction, where people get to bid on very extravagant items and experiences. Do you think Kelly would be willing to donate, you know, a surf lesson or something?"

I said, "I'll ask him and get back to you."

Well, it turns out this charity event was the Monte-Carlo Gala for the Global Ocean, presided by His Serene Highness Albert II, Sovereign Prince of Monaco. Prince Albert and Milutin share a passion for cleaning up the oceans, and this event raises an enormous amount of money and attention for the cause.

When I asked Kelly about donating a surf lesson, he said, "I'll do better than that. I'll donate a day at my surf ranch with one-on-one instruction from me."

Very cool. In 2018 Kelly designed and engineered a solar-powered pool in California that generates the world's longest man-made barrel wave. It is the most highly coveted wave on the planet, rising to eight feet and delivering multiple barrels during a seven hundred-yard ride.

I told Milutin about Kelly's gift to the event, and he said, "You're kidding."

"No, that's what Kelly wants to do."

"Oh my God," Milutin said. "This is incredible. You know, someone will donate fifty thousand dollars for that."

I thought, *Yeah, probably not.*

No offense to Kelly, but nobody was going to donate fifty thousand dollars to ride a man-made wave in the middle of nowhere in central California. Or so I thought...

The opening bid started at—50,000, and the closing bid was—500,000, which was approximately $600,000!!!

Think about that. I was living under a bridge in 2003. I got sober and started making juices and smoothies to get healthy. Then I opened a recovery center, and eventually SunLife Organics, to help others do the same. I met Kelly at SunLife and we became friends. Kelly invited me to Paris for the Ryder Cup charity event, and while we were there I texted my friend Milutin, who invited us to **his** charity event.

Because I got sober and clean on all fronts—body, mind, spirit, intention—and pursued my passion with relentless energy, I was in the humbling position to put two people together with a few text messages. And those few messages ended up bringing in an additional $600,000 to make our beautiful oceans cleaner.

Truly Loving What You Do

I was one of the nearly 300,000 people forced to evacuate because of the incredibly destructive 2018 Woolsey Fire. Thankfully, the firefighters stopped the blaze before it got close enough to do any damage to my home and those around me, but it destroyed over 1,600 structures and killed three people. Several of my dear friends lost everything. Louis Gossett Jr.'s home, where I used to pick up his dogs every day and take them for walks when I was newly sober, is completely gone.

One of my best friends, Dale, whose daughter works at SunLife, lost everything because the day before the fires reached his house they had tented it for termites. They were unable to retrieve even one single item. They literally lost it all.

Even after the fire was finally stopped, my neighbors and I couldn't return to our homes because of the cleanup and unsafe conditions. I still worked though, making the rounds to the SunLife locations to check on employees and customers and help them however I could.

When I stopped at the Pacific Palisades location, I saw people walking around the beautiful new village setting wearing masks so they could breathe. The air was toxic with soot and ash, and there was a palpable sense of sadness and panic. People were frightened.

Then I saw my friend Bart, who owns Bart Baker Insurance Company and happened to be my insurance agent. He was with his wife, and for some reason they were absolutely glowing with joy. I knew their house had been at risk from the fire as well, and I said, "Oh, my God, Bart, are you guys okay?"

"Of course we're okay. We're great."

"So everything's good with your house?

He said, "Oh, I don't know. We haven't been able to find out yet."

I was confused. "What? Why are you doing so great then?"

He said, "We've been handing out checks all morning."

What the hell?

Bart said, "As a matter of fact, are you okay? Do you need anything? Do you need money for a place to stay, or for food and lodging?"

"No, thanks, but I don't need any money."

"What I mean is, your policy with me, it covers being displaced. So if you're staying at a hotel or you need money for food or whatever, I can cut you a check right now."

I said, "You're kidding me."

"No, Khalil, that's the way it works. That's what we do. We've been out since five thirty this morning. We have an emergency triage center where we're cutting checks for people who are displaced."

As he spoke, he grew even happier. He was walking on air. Helping his friends and clients in their time of need had him overflowing with joy and gratitude.

Think about your job.

Or what you **think** you want your job to be.

Are you doing it for the money? The status? Because someone else thinks you should do it?

I have friends who are ridiculously wealthy and equally miserable because of their jobs. One owns a credit card processing company. Another inherited a debt collection agency.

Maybe these are necessary businesses, but they don't seem to be making life better for anyone. They lift no one up, and that includes the owners. They don't seem to be proud of what they do. I can't imagine it brings them joy. But what do I know...

How does your job make you feel? Proud?

Does it set you on fire every day? Fill you with energy and joy?

I'm pretty sure there are insurance agents out there who hate their job and dread work every day. To them I say, "This isn't the path for you."

Then there's Bart, who floats down the sidewalk when he gets a chance to fulfill his purpose and his passion. He's found his path. He truly loves what he does for a living.

If you don't have that now, work to find it. Life is too short to waste time being unnecessarily miserable.

Every day that I wake up and realize I don't have to get a job or go to work, I am absolutely amazed!

Finding Your Purpose

When I was struggling to find my path, I listened to Tony Robbins' Hour of Power every day. The exercises and breathing techniques really resonated with me, and I grabbed onto that ritual and it made a huge difference in my life.

For a complete list of books, podcasts, and other resources that might help you focus on your purpose, go to khalilrafati.com/purpose.

Never stop, never give up! Know it's gonna be hard and sometimes grueling. Know that most will doubt you or talk shit about you. Don't personalize it. Keep going even when it's dark. Look for the good in the world. Keep your prayers simple and your mind sharp and your thoughts positive. Forgive everyone, especially yourself. What is your highest potential?! What is your purpose?! This ain't dress rehearsal. No one can live your dreams for you. This is it. Right here right now!

Passion vs. Purpose

Most people just go to school because that's what they're told.

They get good grades because that's what they're told.

They memorize a bunch of shit and then go to college because that's what they're told.

They memorize a bunch of shit and take out a bunch of loans because that's what they're told.

They get out of college and get a job, any job, because that's what they're told.

Maybe it's a great job, or they feel like it's the best one they can get, so they stay.

Or maybe they chase a better job, more money, more perks, and move around and move around and move around.

But not for what fulfills them.

Not for their purpose.

They stay, or they go, trying to feed that hungry ghost of more, more, more.

More money, more spending, more debt, more misery.

For eleven and a half months out of the year they work toward someone else's dream, neglecting themselves, neglecting their bodies, neglecting their spouses, neglecting their kids.

Never finding their purpose, what fulfills them.

Then, if they're lucky, once or twice a year they go someplace they fantasize about that has a good climate.

They do things they actually love to do, or have been told they should love, for five to seven days.

They spend the majority of the time photographing themselves so they can do some humble bragging on social media.

Knowing all the while that it is completely empty.

And they want to be full.

Maybe they ask themselves, "What's my passion?"

Wrong question.

Ask me what my passion is, and I'll tell you: I'm passionate about shooting speedballs, fame/attention, and eating entire bags of Doritos.

That's not just empty, it will suck the very life and soul out of me.

Instead, ask: "What is my purpose?"

As children we know what fulfills us and what our purpose is. Then adults get ahold of us and society gets ahold of us, and our purpose gets buried under a pile of shit. It gets ignored, neglected, forgotten.

Seek that.

You already know what it is—you just need to remember.

You owe it to yourself and the world.

Passion drains. Purpose fills.

I am a particle of dust.

I am nothing in the grand scheme of things, but at the same time I am a child of God and I was created in God's image.

What a strange paradox to be something so miraculous and great and yet to be nothing at all.

I am floating along on such a beautiful journey, and sometimes it seems like I fought so hard to get to where I am, but then at the same time it seems like I was meant to be here no matter what, and as much as I fought and thrashed in the river of life I was carried along on a very specific journey.

"Every spirit builds itself a house; and beyond its house, a world; and beyond its world a heaven. Know then, that the world exists for you: build, therefore, your own world."

—RALPH WALDO EMERSON

Thanksgiving 2005

In 2005 I was still crashing at my sponsor Robbie's house. I had a couple thousand dollars to my name and I carried it with me everywhere I went because I was scared to death of being broke and homeless again. I mean, I technically was homeless because I didn't have a place of my own, but I did have a car and somewhere warm and safe to sleep.

I was lucky enough to be invited to a Thanksgiving dinner party in Santa Monica, and the house was amazing. It was the kind of place where I tried to act cool, but the whole time my brain was going, "This place is too fancy for you. These people are too fancy for you. The food is too fancy for you." But everyone was incredibly nice and generous and I had a wonderful time.

I left around ten o'clock at night and headed back into Malibu. It was an unusually cold November in Southern California that year so I had the heat blasting, and as I was driving down Wilshire Boulevard feeling warm in my post-party glow I saw people sleeping in doorways.

My heart broke. I started counting people—ten, eleven, twelve—and my car just pulled itself over. I got out of the car and pulled all of the money I had in the world out of my pocket. It wasn't a conscious thought. I just started moving and kept going.

I walked up to every person I saw, handed them a twenty dollar bill, and walked away. Some of them were asleep, and I had to tuck the money into a pocket or under a hand.

I didn't speak to anyone or even make eye contact. I didn't want or deserve any thanks, and my heart wouldn't be able to take it anyway. When everyone I could see had twenty dollars I got back in my car and drove away.

Within a block my body was flooded with euphoria. I felt so high. The wheels of my car weren't touching the ground. It felt like I was floating down the road.

I had a huge grin on my face and then, without warning, sheets of tears poured from my eyes. I cried and cried, tears and sobs and gasps of pure gratitude. Pure love. Love for those people, love for my God, and love for myself.

The only other time I've told that story is to a few 12-step sponsors and people I was sponsoring to show them how good it can feel to implement acts of unconditional love and generosity.

We've all been duped. We've been lied to and will continue being lied to from the cradle to the grave.

Our entire schooling system was created during the industrial revolution to turn children into good factory workers and compliant obedient citizens. Did you ever get in trouble for writing poetry or drawing during class? I sure did. And I find it comical because that's exactly what you're supposed to do as a kid and a human being—you're supposed to create!

We got punished for creating. Think about that for a moment. How about joking around or writing notes to one another or maybe even flirting with the girls or guys who sat near you? I was constantly yelled at and punished for these actions.

They made me wear an actual dunce hat and stand with my face in the corner so other kids in the classroom could laugh at me. Can you imagine? I was doing exactly what I was supposed to be doing as a growing human. Learning to communicate, striving to become liked and accepted and popular.

Do you know what would happen to a human being ten thousand years ago if they were not liked or accepted by the tribe? They didn't eat! Food was not shared with them and oftentimes they would be abandoned by the group, left to starve alone in the wilderness.

We were hunters and gatherers and one of our primary instincts was societal, the desire to be liked and accepted by others. When we are children we play. We imagine and fantasize and create. We take sticks and pretend they're horses and ride them. We take rocks and pretend they're race cars.

We imagine ourselves as superheroes because we are young particles of God created by God in God's image and that's what God does, God creates! A child encouraged to play and draw and create and be what we call artistic is how Picasso and Leonardo da Vinci and Michelangelo became who and what they were.

I saw it. I saw it with my own eyes and felt it with my own hands. I smelled it and I heard it. The intoxicating aroma of flowers permeated the entire countryside. I slept under the same stars.

I stayed in a 1300-year-old monastery that had been converted into a hotel. It didn't matter that the place was remodeled with modern fixtures and electricity and air conditioning. It was still the same building, and I could feel the millions upon millions of prayers that were prayed there.

The austerity, the piety, the devotion. I could smell it through the halls as I walked to my room. When I went to the museum the next morning my mouth kept dropping open, and for the first time in my life I understood the saying "jaw-dropping experience." My mouth literally fell open. Sometimes a gasp followed. I had one moment when I was standing really close to one of Leonardo da Vinci's paintings, and I felt a bolt of energy that hit me right in my sternum. It shot through my entire body and made the hair on my neck and arms stand at attention!

We are supposed to create. That's what we are put on this planet, in this realm of existence, to do. And yet everything we go through as young children and young adults in our so-called schooling system teaches us to do exactly the opposite of create!

We are taught to be quiet and be obedient.

We are taught to get up and stand in line just to go to the bathroom! I clearly remember kids who had to use the bathroom and kept raising their hands, begging the teacher, but the teacher wouldn't let them go so they had an accident. Several times I wasn't allowed to go to the bathroom and sat in agonizing pain, holding it in, causing untold damage to my young developing kidneys and reproductive system and body.

I was constantly punished, made to stand in the corner, made to stand outside of the classroom in the hall. I had my hands smacked over and over again with rulers. Marched down to the principal's office and beaten repeatedly with a giant wooden paddle.

I was held back in sixth grade for disciplinary reasons. I faced a devastating amount of embarrassment and shame when all of my classmates began seventh grade and I remained behind, not because I wasn't smart enough, but because I wouldn't listen.

They did their best to instill fear in me. They did their best to instill shame in me. They did their best to make me feel less than and unworthy, adding to the full dose I was already getting at home.

It's a miracle I made it through all of that without ending up worse off than I did.

Breaking Loose

In the beginning of 2007 I was still sleeping in Robbie's spare room and essentially living out of my car. I had twenty thousand dollars to my name, by far the most money I'd ever possessed at one time. And I mean possessed—I kept it wrapped in a rubber band under Robbie's bathroom sink because I was terrified of not being able to access it at any time.

I was paranoid about going broke again. I needed to see the money, feel it, take it out and count it. I counted it every day. It was incredibly surreal to have that much cash in my hands when I had always been poor.

I was still newly sober and working hard not just to earn money, but to keep from relapsing. I was starting to find real progress in solitude, and every now and then I needed to get away from everything and everyone and just be alone. I needed to reflect, recharge, sit with the silence and try to get my mind to do the same.

On one of these trips I grabbed my cash and drove north on Highway 1. After passing Ventura and Santa Barbara I became hypnotized by the road. About three hours later I was driving through San Simeon, a glorious, majestic stretch of coastal land approaching a little town called Gorda.

The roads around Gorda have these insane hairpin turns, and I was coming around one of them when I saw a truck and trailer parked on the opposite shoulder with the hazards on. The rear tire on the truck was completely flat, and the driver was walking toward it with a jack and tire iron in his hands. He had to be in his seventies, if not older.

I pulled over to help. Not because I'm a good guy or anything, but because I'm from Ohio, and back there, when you see someone having trouble on the side of the road, you stop and help if you can. So I turned on my hazards, looked both ways, and ran across the highway.

"How you doing?" I said.

The old man turned. He seemed surprised to see someone standing next to the flat tire with him.

"Oh, I'm okay. But I can't seem to get the lug nuts loose."

I said, "Oh, no problem. Here, let's see that tire iron."

Now, I had changed a tire before, but it had been quite a few years. There was so much rust around those lugnuts they looked like they were fused to the rim. I wasn't exactly sure what to do next, but I slapped the tire iron on one of the lug nuts and gave it a tug.

Nothing. Not even a squeak.

"I tried spraying some WD-40," the old man said, "but those things are being really stubborn."

I heaved and pushed and pulled, giving it everything I had, and that lugnut didn't budge. Then, in what was either a stroke of brilliance or a mild temper tantrum, I put the handle of the tire iron parallel to the ground and stomped on it.

Success!

It broke loose, and I started laughing with joy and relief, then the old man joined me, and we stood there laughing like a couple of lunatics at this loose, rusty lug nut. I kicked the rest of them loose and we jacked the truck up, changed the tire, and reversed the process to retighten the lugs. I made absolutely sure they were tight—I didn't want this poor guy driving around the hairpins and getting passed by his own loose wheel.

We got the jack and tire iron put away and I said, "You're all set. Have a great day."

"Wait a second," he said, and reached into his pocket for some money.

I said, "No, no, no."

"Oh, I insist."

I didn't know what to do. There was no way I was going to take his money, but I didn't want to offend him. I looked at the ground, embarrassed because I couldn't think of a way to let him know I didn't want or expect anything in return for helping with his tire.

Then from somewhere, or someone, I found the words.

"I don't need the money. I have more money than I know what to do with."

The hair on the back of my neck stood up. My arms broke out in goosebumps. It was the most profound and powerful statement I've ever said in my life. It shot through me like a bolt of lightning.

As soon as I said those words I went from being embarrassed and looking at the ground to holding my head up and looking him straight in the eye. I hadn't looked into his eyes until that moment.

They were a brilliant shade of blue. He looked back at me and from his eyes came light, and energy, and in that moment God stood before me. I saw God.

I know it sounds crazy, like some weird childhood fantasy. However, from that statement, from declaring I had enough and I had faith that I would never need again, God came to me. That man and those blue eyes healed my heart. They healed my poverty mentality, my belief that I was always going to be poor.

In that moment was the shift. Was it the man and his piercing blue eyes? Was it simply me speaking consciously and clearly to my subconscious after so many hours being hypnotized by the road?

I have no idea.

But in that moment, I shifted from scarcity to abundance. I opened myself up to the abundance and prosperity of the universe.

I was no longer a slave to money.

I was no longer a victim of money.

I was in charge of money, and I would make demands on money instead of letting money make demands on me.

We smiled and nodded at each other once more. Then I got in my car and drove away, awestruck and speechless. For the next two days, the only time I spoke was to order food when I stopped to eat.

It was one of the most profound spiritual experiences of my life, and it happened because I stopped to help someone on the side of the road.

The opportunities for generosity and growth are all around us. I don't know if, or how, or when your paradigm shift will happen. But we are all in this together and I constantly ask myself, "How can I help? How can I be of use? How can I be of service?"

RELATIONSHIPS

Communication & Negotiation

This entire book is about the power of change. It's about figuring out exactly what you want and making the changes—both large and small—necessary to get it.

The figuring out part can be hard sometimes. Maybe you already have money, or don't care about money, and you have a loving family and a great group of friends and a job you love, but you're still unfulfilled.

There's something missing.

I can't tell you what that something is.

Only you can identify it. Even if I could, it wouldn't matter.

Other people can bang on you all day about how you need to start painting, open your own business, get healthy—whatever your thing is—but it won't make a bit of difference until you identify it, accept it, and want to make the necessary changes.

Getting to that point is a huge step.

But what comes next can be even harder: Telling people what you want.

The ability to clearly and honestly communicate with other people about what you want is one of the most underrated and under-taught skills in the world.

And I'm not talking about going to UCLA and getting a degree in Communications, because I've tried and failed to wrap my head around what that means. I know a lot of people who have degrees in Communications and can hardly communicate at all.

I'm talking about the raw, unfiltered expression of exactly what you want for yourself in this short, precious life.

Most of us are people pleasers walking through life afraid to ask for what we want because we might hurt someone's feelings or might get rejected.

I'm too selfish.

I don't want to burden other people with what I want.

I don't really need it...

Bullshit bullshit bullshit.

But here's the raw, unfiltered truth: If you don't communicate what you want, who will?

Nothing against other people, they're mostly good, but they have their own shit to deal with. And how ridiculous is it to surrender our ability to get what we want, our happiness, our potential, our **lives**, to someone else?

Would you let a car salesperson choose the car you're going to drive? Or a real estate broker choose the house you're going to live in?

My guess is no.

And yet we let our parents, partners, and society dictate who we are and what we want.

Why?

Because it's easier?

It doesn't offend anyone?

Except your entire bloodline and the limitless forces in the universe working together to bring you into existence in this moment to fulfill your purpose and potential.

But you don't want to be a burden or seem selfish, so you keep your mouth shut and don't tell anyone what you really want?!!!

GOD DID NOT CREATE YOU TO FIT IN.

Fitting in makes you miserable and forces people around you to read your mind, which never works and leads to more disappointment and misery.

Repeat that cycle until the people who love you will do anything to make you happy, if they only knew what you really wanted.

Here's the thing: The greatest value you can offer another person is to tell them the absolute truth.

You're letting them know, "Hey, this is me, as honest and vulnerable as it gets, and

I have faith you can handle it."

And if they can't, who cares? It's only because they have their own shit to work through, or some issue with your truth that has absolutely nothing to do with you.

Now, we're talking about communication, so let's be absolutely clear. Telling the truth about what you want doesn't mean walking up to friends and strangers and saying, "You talk too loud, I want you to be quiet. You're fat, I want you to lose weight. Your shirt stinks, I want you to change."

Those things may be true, but they are not your truth. They're just you expressing yourself as an asshole. They are things that irritate you, or go against how you think things should be. Your expectations for the world.

Nobody is responsible for fulfilling your expectations except you.

SunLife Organics started offering lattes in 2017, and while shopping around for equipment I was shocked to learn a quality milk steamer goes for around $3,000. We started with a few stores, and when the lattes were a hit we spent about 30K putting steamers into all of our locations.

But then the steamers started breaking down. We'd get one fixed and another would break. This became so common and such a time-suck, calling the steamer company and scheduling a technician to come out, I had to delegate management of steamer repairs to one of my employees.

In hindsight, I made a mistake. I wanted to offload the hassle of steamer repairs more than I wanted to make sure the person I handed it off to was:

1. The right person
2. Positioned to succeed

Now, the person who took over the task is a great guy and an extremely hard worker, but at the time he struggled with clearly communicating what he wanted. He was much more concerned with pleasing others and making sure they were comfortable than getting what he wanted.

And sometimes that's okay.

But when pleasing someone else means you get the exact **opposite** of what you want, that's unacceptable. And that's precisely what was going on when he called me from our Cross Creek location, which is not where he should have been.

"Why are you at Cross Creek?" I asked.

"Well, I found out the steamer here has been broken for a couple of weeks. And the customers are getting mad."

"Why would the steamer be broken for a couple of weeks?"

He said, "You know, the steamers, you have to take them in. The company doesn't come out. They don't service them."

"Yes, they do," I said. "Every one of those steamers is under warranty. We just bought them. It's been less than a year."

He said, "Well, they won't come out. I have to take this one in to get it fixed."

I took a deep breath. "Do you remember when we had the frozen yogurt machines? Do you remember how many times you saw one of those guys come out and fix those?"

"Yeah, all the time."

I said, "Yeah, and you know how much they charged us?"

"No."

"Nothing."

And I explained to him, when I called the company and told them I was interested in buying one of their frozen yogurt machines I asked these questions:

"What's the warranty on these?"

"Do you guys come and service them?"

"Do you have a local serviceman who can show up within a day's notice?"

They answered "Yes" to every question.

I said, "Great, can I get that in writing?"

"Absolutely."

So I bought those frozen yogurt machines and anytime something went wrong, especially during that first year, I called them up.

But even after that, even in the second, third, and fourth years, when a machine broke down I called the company and said, "Hey, this is not cool. This machine is only a couple of years old. Why is it breaking down like this?"

And over and over again, they sent somebody out.

I asked my employee, "Do you see what I'm getting at?"

"Yeah, I do."

"Look man, if you don't ask for what you want, you're not going to get it. And now you're driving to Cross Creek to pick up the steamer, taking it across the valley to the repair shop, waiting for two days, then picking it up and taking it back to our store. All while we're serving hundreds of people a day and telling some of them 'Sorry, our steamer is broken.' This is not what we want, brother."

"Yeah. You're right. This is my fault."

I could tell he was getting down on himself. As a people pleaser, a worst-case scenario was coming true for him: I was not pleased.

But I said, "You're right, it is your fault. You didn't clearly communicate what you wanted. But it's not necessarily your fault that you don't know how to do that. Nobody ever taught you. And that is **my** fault."

"Where did you learn it? In school?"

I had to laugh. "Dude, I learned my best communication skills trying to score drugs at three in the morning in neighborhoods with astronomical murder rates. If you didn't say exactly what you wanted and demand that you get it, you might get robbed, beaten, or killed."

He was silent.

"I'm not saying that's how you should learn how to communicate! I'm happier than hell you never went through any of that garbage. But I definitely didn't learn how to communicate in school."

I reminded him:

I didn't finish high school.

I never went to college.

There is nothing special about me.

I simply know myself.

I know my story, my strengths, and my weaknesses.

I know what I want and how to communicate it with honesty and clarity.

There is nothing wrong about asking for what you want.

I told my employee another story, one I picked intentionally. It didn't have to do with SunLife—I wanted to show him how clear communication, and asking for what you want, is vital for all interactions in life, not just work.

At this point in time I was having my home remodeled. It's a small place, about 1,800 square feet, and I was putting in everything I'd ever wanted. This was my sacred space, and I wanted it to be perfect.

When I was ready to start picking appliances I went into a store in the Valley. I didn't walk in with my chest puffed out or slam my fist on the counter and demand to be respected. I smiled. I laughed with the people working there. I asked a ton of questions. I made jokes, but I was clear and honest.

"Look, I don't want to shop around. I don't want to go to a bunch of different places. I don't want to find out I could have gotten this refrigerator cheaper, this oven cheaper. I want you to give me the best prices. I don't want to haggle."

I showed him the list of the items I wanted and asked, "What is this gonna cost?"

They offered me a substantial discount. They gave me free installation. They gave me an extended warranty.

So when the time came for me to buy more appliances, guess where I went?

I went back and got one of those fancy Japanese toilets that rinse your undercarriage. I got a steam shower, a sink, and an outdoor shower.

I bought pretty much every appliance and fixture in my house from them.

We were both getting what we wanted. I got great service and prices on exactly what I wanted in my home, and they got a loyal customer who would bring return business and tell my friends where they should go for their appliances. Everything was perfect.

Until it wasn't.

Five weeks later, I got a call from my general contractor Joe, who was at my house.

"We got a big problem. A big, big problem."

I steeled myself for the worst and said, "What's going on?"

"I needed that sink delivered today so we can measure the marble countertop. Without the sink, we can't cut the marble."

"Okay, so where's the sink?"

Joe said, "I called the appliance center, and the only one they have is cracked. They don't have any more."

"They don't have any more sinks?"

"Not the one you bought. The whole job here is on hold until they can get one."

"When can they get one?" I said.

"Four to six weeks."

"Four to six weeks?! What did you say to them?"

"What could I say? They don't have any more sinks."

I said, "So you're just going to accept that?"

"Khalil, it's the truth. That's the reality."

I said, "Joe, they will be calling you back very soon with a solution."

"How do you figure?"

I said, "Trust me."

I called the appliance center and asked for one of the guys who helped me with the list. First, I wanted to make sure the information I had was correct.

"You told my general contractor that the sink was cracked?"

He said, "Yeah. Let me tell you about that."

Then he started telling me about the cracked sink, how it happened, and other sinks they had available.

I stopped him. "No, no, no. I appreciate all of that, but here's what I want. Even if you have to create the sink, I need you to call my general contractor back right now and give him a solution. I bought every one of my appliances and fixtures from you because of your amazing service, and this is unacceptable."

He said, "I understand. You are absolutely right and I'm sorry about that. I will handle it."

Ten minutes later Joe called me back. "What did you do?"

I said, "What do you mean?"

"The appliance center just called and said they're literally driving over to their competitor's to buy a sink, then they're going to deliver it here."

"Oh, great."

"How did you make them do that?"

I said, "I told them the truth. The truth is, I'm a great, loyal customer and they needed to fix the problem, and they did."

"Did you scream at them?"

"No, man. I didn't yell, I wasn't a dick, and I wasn't rude. I just told them the truth."

Joe said, "Wow, that's amazing."

I didn't think of it as amazing. It made perfect sense to me. But I realized for some people, asking for what you want and getting it is amazing. It's almost unthinkable. It's like some form of magic.

That's why I told the story to my employee, and that's why I put it in this book.

It's not amazing.

It's communicating.

It's telling the truth.

Telling Others What You Want

A lot goes into clear communication and telling others what you want in a way that resonates with them.

You might not be able to use the same words and tone with your parents or kids that you use with your employees or boss.

Awareness is a huge part of this. Reading the room, noticing body language, considering who you're talking to, their goals, expectations, and what story they tell themselves—all of this goes into being aware of the situation, the people involved, and communicating accordingly.

You are not **responsible** for catering to anyone's goals, expectations, or story. But you must realize there are situations that may require doing so to get what you want.

With my sales representative at the appliance center, I knew his goal was to keep me as a happy customer. And I wanted to remain a happy customer. So our goals aligned. But that's as far as it went.

He obviously wasn't considering my expectations and story, which were along the lines of, "I need a countertop, and to get that I need a sink, and there's no way I'm waiting two months to get it."

One of us needed to adjust.

Once I made it clear that I was unhappy and would absolutely take my business elsewhere if the problem wasn't solved, he had to adjust his narrative. He was free to do whatever it took to achieve his goal, including driving to his competitor, buying the sink and delivering it that day. And I remain a happy customer because of it.

And like I told my employee, I didn't learn these critical skills in school. I was forced to learn them for survival. Not economic or entrepreneurial survival—I mean literal survival. Life and death.

I tell a story in *I Forgot to Die* about the time when I purchased my first "boat" of ecstasy, which is one thousand hits. It was also my first time working a transaction with real, hardcore drug dealers instead of my weed dealers, a bunch of Marin County trustafarians. I didn't go into too much detail about the incident, but the line uttered by one of the dealers, "Don't ever bring us twenties again," still sends chills down my spine.

After a series of phone calls directing me from place to place to make sure I wasn't bringing a bunch of S.W.A.T. guys with me, they told me to drive to a specified location and wait. I did, completely oblivious of the stakes and expectations.

I was alone, unarmed, and no one knew where I was. I had $8,000 in twenties because we'd been going to raves and selling ecstasy for twenty a hit, and now I had this big brown paper bag of bills and thought I was ready to step up into the major leagues. I was dead wrong.

A group of men in heavy parkas surrounded my car and told me to get out. They led me into a dark, cold tenement and took me up the stairs to a room where the man in charge was waiting.

He looked at the money and said, "What the fuck is this?"

I thought it was cool. More bills looks like more money, right? Fat stacks.

Well, to a drug dealer, where every second during a deal means exposure, and more cash to count means more time and a greater chance of getting busted or shot, my big bag of bills was a fucked-up rookie mistake.

He stood over the money and stared at me. I'll never forget the feeling of dread I got from that look. He didn't say a word, but his eyes said, "Man, I should beat the shit out of you."

The guys in the parkas surrounded me.

After what seemed like a decade, the man in charge said, "Go down to your car. We'll bring your shit when it's ready. We gotta count all these fucking twenties."

I walked down the cold stairway and got into my car and waited. I tried to act cool, like we were all part of this sexy, glamorous drug deal and everything was fine, but I was freaking out inside.

I almost shit myself.

They could have killed me and taken my car, and no one would ever know what happened to me.

All because I wasn't aware of the expectations and goals of the people I was dealing with.

Now, this was not a scenario to demand customer satisfaction. This wasn't a sink being delayed by my supplier in the Valley. This was one thousand hits of ecstasy from a group of gang members. If they came out with half of the boat and told me they were charging a dumbass tax, I would have thanked them and driven away as fast as possible.

When the guys in parkas finally emerged from the tenement I was ready to bolt. One of them walked up to the driver's window with one hand in his pocket and gestured for me to roll the window down. I did, fully expecting a gun to come out with his other hand.

He pulled out the boat of ecstasy and dropped it in my lap.

"Don't ever bring us twenties again."

Meaning, if you do, you aren't walking out of that room upstairs.

He walked away and I drove away, grateful to be alive.

Which, technically, made me a happy customer. I was also a scared shitless customer.

And I absolutely changed my expectations and goals. I'd like to tell you I never went into that room, or any room like it, again. But that's not true. I did, many times.

But I was prepared, thanks to clear communication.

I never went alone. I never went unarmed.

And I sure as hell never went with twenties.

Total transparency is paramount during the initial stage of any relationship.

It's the foundation upon which the entire relationship is built.

If you begin with honesty and transparency, your foundation will be strong. The relationship can grow with a stable base.

If you begin with lies and deceit, your foundation will be weak. The relationship will likely collapse. Whether it can—or should—be salvaged from the debris depends on how willing you are to be transparent.

If all you really want is to get married, but you lie to your partner and say it's totally fine to keep things casual with no vision of your future together, you're in for some trouble.

If you love strippers and pornography but pretend you like going to church on Sundays so you can have sex with somebody, that relationship is doomed to fail.

And if you don't care, because all you wanted was the sex anyway...please stick to the strippers and pornography and stop wreaking havoc upon others until you're ready and willing to be transparent with yourself about what you are.

Transparency, friendship, and emotional intimacy equal love.

The hotness of your partner doesn't matter when your dog dies.

Amazing sex is a bonus, but it won't help when your parents get dementia and need to be placed in a nursing home.

You're gonna freak out when you hit 30 whether you like it or not.

If you're lucky you'll hit 40 and you'll begin to question everything and everyone and wonder what kind of a legacy you want to leave behind.

If you're really lucky, you're gonna hit 50 and in some way, large or small, you're going to have a midlife crisis and most likely freak the fuck out.

When that freakout happens you might choose to buy a Porsche. Or you might choose to sell your belongings and turn to a life of philanthropy and charity.

Either way, having an amazing partner at your side who truly knows you, loves you, and accepts you for who you really are will ultimately be the only thing that matters.

Love is the quiet acceptance and understanding of another person's imperfections.

It's your responsibility to be transparent with your imperfections.

Period.

From Skid Row Bluff to Marin County Truth

That boat of ecstasy seems like a luxury yacht compared to where things went from there. By 2001 my girlfriend Sam and I had gone from living in an apartment on the ocean to sleeping in our car so we could afford to buy heroin. Not to sell—this was strictly to keep us getting high, what we ironically called "getting well."

When she went into treatment, I lost everything. The bank account and car were both in her name, so I didn't have access to money or a place to sleep. I was homeless.

Because I was resourceful I quickly jumped on welfare, food stamps and hotel vouchers. I got a hotel room on Skid Row, which for a kid from Ohio somehow seemed glamorous and cool. Like I was part of some Hollywood story.

That did not last.

At the time, Skid Row was fairly safe during the day. Your chances of getting stabbed or thrown out a twelfth-floor window were pretty slim.

But when the sun went down, it got scary. And the later it got, the more dangerous the area and people in it became.

There's the saying, "Nothing good happens after midnight." Well, it was about two in the morning, and I was trying to buy crack at Fifth and Spring, a terrifying place to be. Now it's gentrified with condos and juice bars, but back then it felt like one of Dante's concentric circles of Hell.

I had a couple hundred dollars in my pocket thanks to my mom and Western

Union. I was looking to buy forty dollars' worth of crack, and I found a guy standing on the sidewalk who had what I wanted. It should have been a simple transaction: I give him two twenties and he gives me the rocks, then we go our separate ways and everyone is happy. Well, as happy as an addict and dealer on Skid Row can be.

But, because I was high and stupid, I pulled out the entire wad of cash and started to peel off the bills.

"No, no, hold up," the guy said. "We got it over here. Over here."

He put his arm around me and guided me toward an open doorway. I went, because again: high and stupid.

There was a group of people inside the doorway and it was immediately obvious, even to me, that they were going to rob me. One of them held a knife. I knew that even if I gave up my cash without a fight, there was a good chance I was going to get beaten, stabbed, or killed.

I yelled, "Back off motherfuckers!"

I blasted them with the wild and crazy eyes of a strung-out crack addict and reached under my shirt to my waistband, where I had absolutely nothing hidden. I bluffed.

It was straight out of The Godfather, when Michael Corleone and Enzo the baker stood outside the hospital and scared off the would-be hitmen sent to kill Vito Corleone. I had used the tactic once before in Tijuana when a group of Ketamine dealers tried to rob me and my girlfriend at the time.

I yelled again, "Back off!"

A few of them bolted, in a panic to get away from this madman. The rest froze. I don't know if they believed I had a weapon or not, but they weren't prepared to call my bluff.

I backed away and ran down the sidewalk as fast as my skinny little crack legs would carry me.

This is obviously an extreme example of bluffing. There is a slight difference in stakes between negotiating a lease or the price of bulk bananas and trying to buy crack on Skid Row. But the same concept still applies and is used by people doing business every single day.

And yes, there are still times when my insecurities creep up and try to convince me I'm a nobody, a nothing, an imposter, and I don't deserve to be in the room with the people I'm negotiating with.

This happened when I finally got the chance to sit down with a property owner I'd been chasing for three years, calling and emailing and getting nowhere. Then I discovered my friend Matt knew him, and I begged for five minutes of his time. It worked.

You know that "Oh shit" feeling when you finally get something you've wanted for years, and realize you'd better not screw it up?

Yeah, that happened.

I mean, this guy is a visionary genius. He has properties all over California and he curates them to be community spaces where art, culture and commerce can all flourish. His properties are a perfect fit for SunLife.

But why should he care about that? He didn't need me or SunLife. He had hundreds of business owners begging to get a lease with him, and they'd all pay more than we could afford. I knew going into the meeting he had all the leverage.

To make things worse, when Matt took me to the meeting he said, "He has ten minutes for you. Then he has a meeting with Charlie Munger."

As in, *the* Charlie Munger who works with Warren Buffet.

I was stunned. "How the hell does he get a meeting with Charlie Munger?"

Matt said, "Oh, they're business partners."

Cue the flop sweat.

"Okay," Matt said. "He's ready. Remember: ten minutes."

Ten minutes isn't enough time for a bluff. It's barely enough time to tell him what SunLife Organics is. So I spent three minutes pitching myself and the brand of SunLife, then went for the big ask, and I was completely honest about what I wanted.

"Look, I love what you're doing here in Montecito. But what I'd really love to do is come up and meet you at your Marin location because that is the Holy Grail. That's where I want to be."

Then I shut up and waited for what seemed like an hour, but was actually about two seconds.

He said, "Yeah, sure. Come on up. I got to go."

And he left, to meet with Charlie Munger.

But he'd agreed to a second meeting with me, and I was thrilled. It wasn't a flat-out "No", so I considered it a huge win. A month later I flew up to San Francisco and took an Uber to the Marin County Country Mart. When I got there I texted the landlord, and he wrote back, "I'm just finishing up lunch, I'll meet you at 1 p.m."

As I waited, I had crazy last-second doubts about how to communicate with this guy. My ego wanted me to boast and bluff, talk about all the celebrities who come to SunLife, how much everybody loves us, and how lucky he'd be to have us on his property.

But my gut told me to just be honest. Be transparent. This guy heard countless pitches every month. I wasn't going to bluff him. I wasn't going to impress him. He was partners with Charlie Munger—I sure as hell wasn't going to blow him away with our spreadsheets.

I kept coming back to why I wanted to work with this man and be in his locations: Because he cares. He creates business ecosystems that thrive along with the surrounding communities. He doesn't just want a warm body with a checkbook as a tenant like most landlords. He is a curator and tries to provide value for the people he serves. Just like me.

He walked in and said, "I only have a few minutes, so we have to be brief. What do you have in mind?"

A few minutes?! I thought I had ten!

I started freaking out again. Then I took a deep breath and said, "What you have created here, it's absolutely amazing. This is the coolest thing I've ever seen, and I would be so honored and so thrilled if you would consider allowing me to put my brand in this location."

No bluff, no leverage. Just clear, honest communication.

I only had a few minutes, so I wanted to make sure he understood exactly what I wanted and why.

An hour and a half later we were still talking. He said to me. "Don't take the ferry back to San Francisco. I'll drive you."

We spent another hour in his car while he gave me a tour of San Francisco, which was incredibly generous of him.

Clear, honest communication took us from a few minutes to over two and a half hours of wonderful connection. Three weeks later we had a lease deal on the table.

Now, does this always work so well?

Hell no. My honesty and transparency has gotten me laughed out of rooms many times. I've been called an idiot who has no idea what I'm talking about.

But that's fine. Whether they intend to or not, those people are communicating just as honestly as I am, and they make it very clear we aren't a good fit for each other. I don't want to work with anyone who laughs another person out of the room or calls them an idiot.

Sometimes I forget how truly blessed and lucky I am.

I forget how kind and loving God is.

I made such a complete and horrible mess of my life, but the moment I got on my knees and asked for forgiveness I was forgiven.

My prayer asking for forgiveness was answered, and the thousands of prayers since then have been answered, too.

Not necessarily in the order and fashion I imagined, but answered nonetheless with grace, kindness and love!

If you are not living the life that you feel you should be living, please know you can start over at any time.

The power and grace of God are far greater than any of us could ever fathom!

January 15th, 2003

In 2017 I was at my USC SunLife Organics location and a couple L.A.P.D. officers came in to order some smoothies.

I rushed over to the register and told my team, "Whatever these guys want, it's on the house."

The officers were a little shocked, but graciously accepted.

I told them, "Any time law enforcement or first responders come into my store while I'm there, it's comped."

"That's great," one of them said. "But...why?"

"Because an L.A.P.D. officer saved my life. I used to be a homeless drug addict."

They looked at me, all clean-shaven, happy and healthy in my expensive clothes, wearing my ridiculous watch.

Then they cracked up.

"Bullshit," one of them said.

So I told them about how on January 15th of 2003 I was arrested at 11:20 p.m. on Washington and La Brea. If you've read *I Forgot to Die*, you may recall the unique exchange between Officer Dmitri and me.

I was high on crack cocaine, hadn't slept for forty-five days, and was convinced someone was trying to kill me. So when I saw a police cruiser parked near a convenience store I dove into the back seat for protection.

Needless to say the officers were a bit startled.

When they pulled me out I tried to destroy the only evidence I had on me—an empty crack pipe—but when I threw it down onto the asphalt it just bounced. The officers and I stared at it for a moment, then they laughed.

I'd made a complete fool out of myself and the officers, even though they were busy being brave and solid souls putting their lives on the line night after night, had the compassion and patience to see I needed help, not enforcement.

Officer Dmitri was especially compassionate. Even though he could have just sent me on my way or busted me on the spot with no questions asked, he seemed genuinely curious about my situation.

He asked where I was from, where I lived, why I was homeless. I was shocked that the questions came from a place of concern instead of feeling like an interrogation.

Then came the punchline.

Officer Dmitri said, "You seem like a good guy. Why don't you get your shit together?"

Oh no, I thought. *A Come-to-Jesus talk. Just arrest me, please.*

I was not in the mood for a lecture. In my condition, any kind of judgement or holier-than-thou attitude was like scalding water on my filthy skin.

He persisted, telling me I should get clean and find work and blah blah blah, and he must have recognized what I needed most was to spend some time off the street, because he eventually arrested me.

Officer Dmitri was right to get me off the streets. And while that arrest led to one of the most harrowing experiences of my life, my incarceration at L.A. County Jail and my descent to rock bottom, it also led to my complete surrender.

Without that surrender, I would be dead.

I told the two L.A.P.D. officers that story. Then I reached over and took a copy of *I Forgot to Die* off the shelf and showed them the front—the photo of me weighing 109 lbs. with open sores all over my face.

The one who'd called "Bullshit" grabbed the book and stared at it.

"Holy shit, you're serious, aren't you?"

"Yeah, I'm serious. That was me."

He said, "I want to buy this."

"No, no way. I'm gonna give it to you. Take it."

We shook hands and they left, and I was overjoyed about being in the position to tell that story and treat them to whatever they wanted from the menu.

About a week later I was driving on the 10 Freeway, doing my usual rounds, when my phone rang. I didn't recognize the number but answered anyway.

"Hello?"

"This is Detective Dmitri."

My heart dropped.

I thought, *Oh, shit. What's wrong? What happened?*

I said, "Okay, uh, how can I help you?"

"I'm the guy who arrested you sixteen years ago. I was wondering if we could meet up."

I didn't think I'd heard him correctly.

I said, "Holy shit! Are you fucking kidding me?"

He started laughing. "No, I'm not kidding you."

It turns out the officers who came into the USC location had passed my story around until it reached Detective Dmitri.

I said, "Yes, of course, I would love to meet you! In fact, I've often thought about you and wondered how you are these days."

"Well, I'm working right now. What's your schedule?"

Less than an hour later I was standing behind the register at the USC location when a man in a suit walked in.

I recognized him immediately.

It was the same guy.

It was Officer Dmitri. Now Detective Dmitri.

I came out from behind the counter and we looked at each other, and he started to get choked up.

I reached out to shake his hand and he put his arms out and he hugged me. He held on for a long time.

When he let me go I looked at him and said, "What's wrong?"

"Shit, man, we never get to see this. We never get to see this."

I led him to a table and we sat down.

I said, "What do you mean? Never get to see what?"

As he wiped tears from his eyes, he said, "You have no idea the shit that we witness on a daily basis. The stabbings, shootings, the murders, the overdoses...over and over again. I've been doing this a long time, man, and I never get to see this."

He got emotional again, so of course I got emotional, so we both sat there grinning and crying.

We talked for an hour and I tried my best to get him to eat everything on the menu. We just kept drinking smoothies and eating Açaí bowls and talking and talking and talking.

It was amazing,

I didn't want the conversation to end, but he had to get back to work. We exchanged cell phone numbers and began talking regularly.

Now we talk and text every day. We've developed a deep and meaningful relationship.

One morning while I was vacationing in Maui he texted me, asking if I knew how much money I had to my name when he arrested me.

I wrote back, "No, but I imagine not much."

He sent me a screenshot of the arrest report with the amount circled: $3.50!

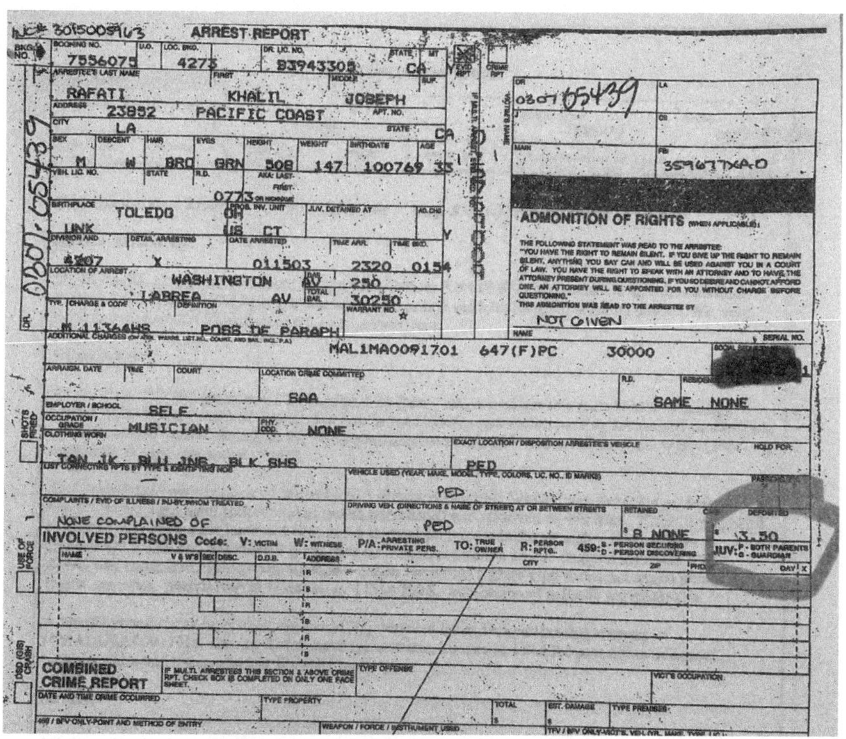

MJC# 3015009163 ARREST REPORT

BKG. NO. Booking No. 7556075 | Loc. Bkg. 4273 | Dr. Lic. No. B3943305 | State CA

Arrestee's Last Name RAFATI | First KHALIL | Middle JOSEPH

Address 23852 PACIFIC COAST | Apt. No.

City LA | State CA

Sex M | Descent W | Hair BRO | Eyes GRN | Height 508 | Weight 147 | Birthdate 100769 | Age 33

Veh. Lic. No. | State | R.D. | AKA: Last- First- | 0773

Birthplace TOLEDO OH | Prob. Inv. Unit | Juv. Detained At

UNK | US | CT

Division and 4207 | Detail Arresting X | Date Arrested 011503 | Time Arr. 2320 | Time Bkd. 0154

Location of Arrest WASHINGTON AV | LABREA AV | Bail 250 | Total Bail 30250

Typ. Charge & Code M 11364HS | Definition POSS OF PARAPH | Warrant No. ★

DR 0807 65439

FBI 359677XA0

ADMONITION OF RIGHTS (WHEN APPLICABLE)

THE FOLLOWING STATEMENT WAS READ TO THE ARRESTEE: "YOU HAVE THE RIGHT TO REMAIN SILENT. IF YOU GIVE UP THE RIGHT TO REMAIN SILENT, ANYTHING YOU SAY CAN AND WILL BE USED AGAINST YOU IN A COURT OF LAW. YOU HAVE THE RIGHT TO SPEAK WITH AN ATTORNEY AND TO HAVE THE ATTORNEY PRESENT DURING QUESTIONING. IF YOU SO DESIRE AND CANNOT AFFORD ONE, AN ATTORNEY WILL BE APPOINTED FOR YOU WITHOUT CHARGE BEFORE QUESTIONING."

THIS ADMONITION WAS READ TO THE ARRESTEE BY NOT GIVEN

Name | Serial No.

Additional Charges MAL1MA0091701 647(F)PC 30000

Arraign. Date | Time | Court | Location Crime Committed SAA | R.D. | Residence SAME NONE

Employer / School SELF

Occupation / Grade MUSICIAN | Phy. Cod. NONE

Clothing Worn TAN JK BLU JNS BLK SHS | Exact Location / Disposition Arrestee's Vehicle PED | Hold For

List Connecting Rpts by Type & Identifying Nos. — | Vehicle Used (Year, Make, Model, Type, Colors, Lic. No., ID Marks) PED

Complaints / Evid of Illness / Injury, Whom Treated NONE COMPLAINED OF | Driving Veh. (Directions & Name of Streets at or Between Streets) PED | Retained $ 8 NONE | Deposited $ 3.50

INVOLVED PERSONS Code: V: VICTIM W: WITNESS P/A: ARRESTING PRIVATE PERS. TO: TRUE OWNER R: PERSON RPTG. 459: S - PERSON SECURING D - PERSON DISCOVERING JUV: P - BOTH PARENTS G - GUARDIAN

Name | V & W's | Sex | Desc. | D.O.B. | Address | City | Zip | Phone | Day | X

COMBINED CRIME REPORT | IF MULTI. ARRESTEES THIS SECTION & ABOVE CRIME RPT. CHECK BOX IS COMPLETED ON ONLY ONE FACE SHEET. | Type Offense | Vict's Occupation

Date and Time Crime Occurred | Type Property | Total $ | Est. Damage $ | Type Premises

459 / BFV Only-Point and Method of Entry | Weapon / Force / Instrument Used | TFV / BFV Only-Vict's. Veh. (Yr., Make, Type, Lic.)

I shuddered when I saw it! There I was, sitting by a gorgeous pool in Hawaii listening to the ocean waves crash below, and that photo took me all the way back to that night when I was thirty-three, homeless and addicted to crack and heroin.

I couldn't believe how much things have changed.

How much I have changed.

And I was so grateful the universe brought me and Dmitri back together.

When he graduated from an elite force of officers after 25 years of service, Dmitri invited me to the ceremony. I was surrounded by close friends and family members of L.A.P.D.'s finest—a setting I never dreamed I'd be in.

The irony of my relationship with Dmitri is not lost on me.

Me, a convicted felon, former drug addict and dealer.

Dmitri, an upstanding member of law enforcement. An amazing father, husband and friend who made all the right choices in life while I was dead-set on making all the wrong choices, determined to not just screw up my own life, but the lives of everyone I knew.

We could not be more opposite, but Dmitri and I realized early on that even though our first meeting found us on opposite sides of the law, we had some extraordinary things in common.

We are both exactly the same age, born in 1969.

Both of our fathers were born in small towns outside of Jerusalem.

Risking a look at the bigger picture, it's an amazing example of how we are all connected in some way, shape or form.

We are all brothers and sisters.

We are all doing the best we can.

Years ago I would have feared and hated Dmitri.

I was doing shit I shouldn't have been doing.

I was breaking the law.

Speeding, driving drunk, selling drugs...just conducting myself like an all-around piece of shit.

And he would have been a threat to me being able to live that way.

Today, I don't live that way.

I have changed.

I live an amazing life.

I have a great business.

I am surrounded by people who love me, and I love them.

And, God forbid, if anything were to ever threaten the way I live, I'm going to ask the police for help.

The same police I used to hate.

I'm so grateful to have woken up.

I'm so grateful for my relationship with Dmitri.

I'm so grateful that after so many years of living like a piece of shit, I was able to turn my life around.

I am so grateful for the change I have gone through.

Yet I have so far to go.

I still make mistakes every single day.

I have to constantly keep my ego in check and try my best not to be an asshole.

You don't just wake up one day and become a better person.

It takes work, and in my experience, it takes daily work.

But I can now finally say, after five decades on this planet, that through the help of so many people I am much closer to being the man that God intended me to be.

Being the son that God intended me to be.

And the friend.

And the neighbor.

If I can make this change, so can you.

Act Natural

You know the old saying that 90% of success is showing up?

Well, just showing up won't cut it anymore. What really matters is how you communicate once you're there.

As a society we are getting worse at interpersonal communication. By that, I mean speaking to another person actually **in person**, looking them in the eye, using your body language to support the words coming out of your mouth. We look down, we mumble, we say "like" every other word because we aren't used to expressing our thoughts as we form them.

Early in my sobriety when I was working at Sherman's Dog Grooming Service, Sherman, the owner, offered to pay for me to take acting lessons. I jumped at the chance, of course, because one of the reasons I'd moved to L.A. was to become a famous movie star. I craved the lights, the attention, the camera.

I did not crave—nor did I expect—the painful humiliation of trying to act in front of that camera and watching the playback with the entire class while the instructor tore our performances apart.

But during those sessions I began to notice the stiffness in my body when I was feeling afraid or insecure. My hands sometimes weren't sure where to go or what to do while I was talking, which I'd never realized before. This went on week after week, month after month.

I eventually forgot about the camera and focused on my mannerisms, my voice and tone. I relaxed. My acting improved a bit, but my ability to communicate with others improved exponentially.

Sherman's mother Teddy taught the class, and she took a real liking to me. After about six months she offered to give me private, one-on-one lessons at her house, and I obviously pounced on the opportunity to improve even more.

Take acting classes whether you want to be an actor or not. It doesn't matter how old you are. Get in front of the camera and start getting scrutinized.

It can absolutely suck, but it's the fastest way I know of to develop great communication skills.

Connection

"For 100 years now, we've been singing war songs about addicts. I think all along we should have been singing love songs to them, because the opposite of addiction is not sobriety. The opposite of addiction is connection."

—JOHANN HARI

I vividly remember being in fourth grade and crying out for help.

For me, that meant picking up a bottle during recess and smashing it on the ground to make the other kids laugh and cheer. As a ten-year-old kid, it made me feel like a rock star.

The next day all the kids gathered around me, and I smashed another bottle. The nuns heard the shattering glass and scurried over.

"Who did that?! Who did that?!"

They couldn't tell who broke the bottle because of the mob of children, all of us feigning innocent ignorance. We had a shared secret, an unbreakable bond. I was part of an elite tribe, a band of classmates, and they were protecting me from punishment because they appreciated my rebellion.

This went on for a few days until, of course, someone told on me.

I obviously didn't realize at the time that I was crying out for help, that I was desperately seeking connection with someone, anyone, anything. We have thousands of generations whispering in our ear that we need to become popular, we need to procreate, we need to provide for our tribe. I was doing what my DNA told me to do. I was just trying to fit in, to be popular, to get people to like me. I'm sure you can remember similar moments from your past, some you're proud of, some...not so much.

But here is why this particular memory is so seared into my being: Nobody else realized I was crying out for help either.

When the nuns found out it was me breaking the bottles, they didn't ask why I felt the need to act out in such a way.

They didn't check with my mother and father about how things were at home.

They didn't send me to the principal's office for reprimanding.

They didn't bring out the paddle, which I would have taken any day over what they did.

They decided on their own that I would no longer be allowed to go outside for recess or eat lunch with the other kids. While my classmates got to enjoy a meal together and the fresh air and sunshine during recess, the nuns took me to the foul, dirty janitor's room with the moldy mops and buckets of chemicals.

I had to sit in there by myself for an hour every day, exiled and ostracized. It was solitary confinement at a crucial, formative point in my life. I needed connection, community, compassion, and instead I got isolation. I felt less than. I felt dirty. I felt disgusting.

I weep for that little boy.

I still struggle to find connection.

If you are feeling alone, you are not alone.

Your isolation is not necessary.

Reach out.

Tell someone you need help.

You don't need to shatter glass, cut yourself, drink yourself numb every day.

You don't need to eat comfort food day and night to numb yourself.

You don't need to drown yourself in countless hours wasted staring at someone else's life on social media.

We are all in this together.

"Humor is tragedy plus time."

—MARK TWAIN

"Happiness is tragedy plus time multiplied by change."

—KHALIL RAFATI

Foreign to Myself

School didn't get much better for me after that janitor's room. I always felt less than. I always felt dumb.

After failing the 6th grade I shut down. I quit doing homework and only went to school sporadically until I got kicked out in 8th grade, then again freshman year.

Ultimately, I dropped out. I just accepted being different and dumb, and feeling dirty wasn't something that was going to change for many decades.

This belief system of inferiority stuck with me into my mid-twenties, when I was washing cars for a living. Then, one day I walked past a movie theater in Santa Monica called Laemmle's 4-Plex. I saw a poster for a movie called *Belle Epoque* with three stunningly beautiful women ravishing a young man.

After staring for a few minutes I walked up to the ticket booth and bought one for the next showing. When the movie started I was very confused—it was in Spanish, and I had to follow along by reading subtitles. I'd always been a slow reader and struggled to keep up, to understand what was happening in the story, but I was captivated. It may have been the first time I actually cared about what I was reading!

I went back multiple times and rewatched the film. More importantly, I reread. They had a constant stream of foreign films at the theater, and my favorite thing became buying a ticket to any random movie without asking what it was about or reading the movie poster. Sometimes the movies were from India, or Pakistan, Japan, Germany, Italy. Every single time I had an incredible experience. I learned about different cultures around the world, how to read and retain information, how to interpret body language.

I discovered the foreign film section at the Blockbuster on Fourth and Montana and rented every title they had, many of them two or three times. *Zentropa*, *The*

Bicycle Thief, Cinema Paridiso, Toto the Hero...These movies not only opened up my mind, but instilled passion in me. A lust for life. My whole world began to open up. My heart opened up.

Soon I jumped from the screen to books: *The Fountainhead*, *Siddhartha*, *Demian*, *The Alchemist*. I developed a hunger to educate myself that could not be satisfied. I fell in love with reading and learning, one of the most precious gifts I've ever been blessed to receive.

Of course, I was also in the midst of struggling with mental illness and addiction, and you've heard me say it before: I'm an addict and always will be. Sometimes my ability to focus a singular, relentless intention on one thing can be beneficial, and I consumed books and knowledge like a starving man at a buffet. I found incredible solace in the quiet introspection that came with reading and feeding my endless curiosity.

As I learned more from films and books and built my own internal library of dialogue, allegory, philosophy, and communication styles, an amazing thing happened:

I stopped feeling inferior.

I didn't feel dumb anymore.

I could carry on a conversation without the voice in my head constantly interrupting to tell me I was going to say something stupid and expose myself as an ignorant, dropout loser from the Midwest.

That voice began to disappear, silenced by the quiet, calm stream of knowledge I slowly amassed.

Knowledge gave me the confidence to communicate.

To speak with my own voice, sing my own song, and dance my own dance.

My teachers always said, “Get your head out of the clouds!”

I’m glad I didn’t listen.

Allow yourself to dream again.

Create the life you’ve always wanted.

Rejoicing

I am now leading the abundant life because I believe in a God of abundance.

I am supplied with everything that contributes to my beauty, wellbeing, progress and peace.

I am experiencing daily the fruits of the Spirit of God within me.

I accept my good now; I walk in the light that all good is mine.

I am peaceful, poised, serene and calm.

I am one with the source of life; all my needs are met at every moment of time and every point of space.

I now bring "all the empty vessels" to the Father within.

The fullness of God is made manifest in all the departments of my life.

"All that the Father hath is mine."

I rejoice that this is so.

BE HERE NOW

"Inside of you there is a hidden being, still in the deep sleep of childhood. Bring it to life! In each one of you there is a call, a will, an impulse of nature, an impulse toward the future, the new, the higher. Let it mature, let it resound, nurture it!"

—HERMANN HESSE

It's better to die a single death than a thousand deaths of regret.

Being Here Now vs. Attaching to Now

When I was addicted to crack, cocaine and heroin I lost everything in my life. I had no job and nowhere to call home. I lost my girlfriend, my roommates, and everything that made me happy.

At least, my definition of **happy** at that time.

I cried and complained about everything I'd lost. I begged my girlfriend to come back to me. I pissed and moaned about the apartment I got evicted from. I raged about how unfair it was that I couldn't afford to score any heroin.

I was miserable, mourning how much I'd lost and wailing about how I would give anything to have it back.

If you tried to inflict any of those things on me today, I'd fight you to the death.

That girlfriend? Enabling, codependent and manipulative.

That gross old apartment?

The drugs and so-called friends?

If you tried to hold me down and shove needles in my body, force me to live among people I can't stand and who can't stand me, I'd fight like a man being dragged to the electric chair.

That life I made for myself was horrible. That **now** I loved so much, that I cried for, which was such a disgusting existence?

It was a noose around my neck, and I pulled furiously on the other end of that rope. The harder I pulled, the more I clung, the more it suffocated me.

What are you clinging to? What **now** are you attached to that needs to be cut loose so you can be free to find your true joy?

The everything of **then** means nothing **now**.

Quiet, alone, still.

No TV to watch, no car to drive, nowhere to go.

Peaceful, content, grateful.

No one to save or rescue, no crisis real or imagined (mostly imagined) to avert, nowhere to be.

Here now, really truly here now.

There is not some destination or circumstance that will make me feel more fulfilled or happy. This is not my house and these are not my things and if they were, it would not change anything. There is nothing I can get or buy or do that will truly alter how I feel inside.

I feel good.

It's not a familiar feeling, but at the core of my being: I feel genuinely good.

It's unfamiliar because I'm always busy being busy and have such a voracious appetite for success, a lot of the time I feel anxious and undone. Underneath those feelings were sadness and regret.

After lots of meditation and contemplation I found the core of these feelings, and they were mostly tied to childhood.

To intellectually know the basis of my unrest, sadness, and anxiety is one thing, but that is far different than actually knowing. Knowing is knowing.

I never allow myself to just be, and if I were running this ship there would be tension, desire, frustration, optimism, planning…

But I am a guest, so there's nothing to do but eat and laugh and contemplate.

Very blessed, very lucky. Looks great in pictures, and it is.

But the real blessing is not the fancy stuff. The real blessing is the time I have allowed myself and the letting go of control.

I always want to control, but that is not possible here. I am literally out of control and at complete peace with it! How strange.

I Am Here Now.

Wooden Floors

When I finally purchased my first home and began remodeling it I had these amazing natural hardwood floors put in. Not laminate—actual solid white oak from Europe.

My girlfriend said, "We should start taking our shoes off inside."

"Ummm..." I said.

For one thing, there was still a lot of construction going on and it wasn't safe to walk around barefoot. But the main reason: I just thought it was stupid. Shoes on, shoes off, it's a hassle and a waste of time.

But as the weeks passed and the construction wrapped up, I found myself waking up and pausing on the edge of my bed with my bare feet on the wooden floor. I started to build a reverence for that moment, the wood, its energy.

Every time my feet touched the floor my reverence grew. I got down and smelled the wood, ran my fingers over the grain, marveled at how strong and resilient the material was. What was happening in the world while that swirl of grain was being formed? That knot?

The tipping point happened after a long day of running around Malibu, Century City, and Pacific Palisades. I got home and jumped in our outdoor sauna, then rinsed off in the shower next to it, and when I walked inside I could smell the natural wood filling our home. My feet were incredibly sensitive from the heat of the sauna and I felt the texture of the planks, every swirl and groove.

I looked down at my shoes resting just inside the door and it hit me. I finally understood. I carried them downstairs and put them on a mat by the door to the garage.

When my girlfriend got home that night, I said, "You were right."

"About what?"

"The shoe thing. We need to take our shoes off when we come inside."

"Yeah? What changed your mind?"

"Cleanliness, for one thing. I ran around all day today, and my shoes are filthy. Who knows what kind of dirt and chemicals I'm tracking around from the sidewalks? The parking lots and ramps? But more important are respect and energy. Those shoes carry the struggles of my day with them. I don't want to bring that energy into our home. And respect for the trees that made these planks. They deserve to be felt and appreciated. So, yeah. I finally get it."

"Good," she said.

As I write this, my bare feet are resting on the wooden floor. The house is quiet. I can feel the energy in the wood and try to put it into my words.

I hope you can feel it and take it with you today.

Nature is as close to God as one can be.

Don't

Don't be afraid to chase the sun.

Don't be afraid to live for yourself.

Don't be afraid to pursue your dreams no matter how silly people think or say they are.

Don't be afraid to be alone—that is where and when we grow.

Don't ever tell yourself that you can't change or that you can't do something.

Don't ever allow the self-defeating voice inside your head to convince you that you are less than what you truly are, that you don't have what it takes.

Don't ever doubt the Almighty Grace of a living, loving God. I laugh when people ask me if I believe in God or I believe in miracles.

Don't compare yourself to others.

Don't let your ego tell you that other people are just lucky, or came from money, or are smarter than you and that's why they have good lives.

Don't be afraid to give yourself everything you've ever wanted.

Let a man radically alter his thoughts, and he will be astonished at the rapid transformation it will effect in the material conditions of his life. Men imagine that thought can be kept secret, but it cannot; it rapidly crystallizes into habit, and habit solidifies into circumstance. Bestial thoughts crystallize into habits of drunkenness and sensuality, which solidify into circumstances of destitution and disease: impure thoughts of every kind crystallize into enervating and confusing habits, which solidify into distracting and adverse circumstances: thoughts of fear, doubt, and indecision crystallize into weak, unmanly, and irresolute habits, which solidify into circumstances of failure, indigence, and slavish dependence: lazy thoughts crystallize into habits of uncleanliness and dishonesty, which solidify into circumstances of foulness and beggary: hateful and condemnatory thoughts crystallize into habits of accusation and violence, which solidify into circumstances of injury and persecution: selfish thoughts of all kinds crystallize into habits of self-seeking, which solidify into circumstances more or less distressing. On the other hand, beautiful thoughts of all kinds crystallize into habits of grace and kindliness, which solidify into genial and sunny circumstances: pure thoughts crystallize into habits of temperance and self-control, which solidify into circumstances of repose and peace: thoughts of courage, self-reliance, and decision crystallize into manly habits, which solidify into circumstances of success, plenty, and freedom: energetic thoughts crystallize into habits of cleanliness and industry, which solidify into circumstances of pleasantness: gentle and forgiving thoughts crystallize into habits of gentleness, which solidify into protective and preservative circumstances: loving and unselfish thoughts crystallize into habits of self-forgetfulness for others, which solidify into circumstances of sure and abiding prosperity and true riches.

A particular train of thought persisted in, be it good or bad, cannot fail to produce its results on the character and circumstances. A man cannot directly choose his circumstances, but he can choose his thoughts, and so indirectly, yet surely, shape his circumstances.

— JAMES ALLEN, *As A Man Thinketh*

Our Two Realities

We live in two realities now.

The reality of what's left of real-world actual relationships and experiences, and the reality of social media where none of us have problems or bad days or even a blemish.

So-called "social" media is a make believe place filled with humblebragging and sarcasm, where we all get to "Live our best lives!"

If my life actually looked like it does on Instagram I'd be a billionaire and my feet would never touch the ground. I would be in a constant state of bliss. I don't post stories of myself curled up in the fetal position on the sofa at 3 a.m., rocking back and forth battling my depression and demons. Or pics of myself crying in the shower because I injured my back again.

I don't write multiple paragraphs on how my giant forehead is getting bigger as I age or how the fat on my belly is gaining momentum.

No, I'm looking for Likes! I'm trying to build self-esteem with an iPhone and filters. I want to be loved and accepted. I want to be a hero!

Don't get me wrong. My life is 10,000 times better now than it was 16 years ago when I was homeless, broke and drinking and drugging with complete abandon. But there are also days like this one, where instead of a restful night it feels like someone threw me in the washing machine without water and hit the start button.

I don't need empathy or sympathy. There are times when I'm going to suffer. PTSD, depression and anxiety are a part of my reality. Suicidal ideation has been around since my early teens, but now only as an infrequent visitor and much less aggressive.

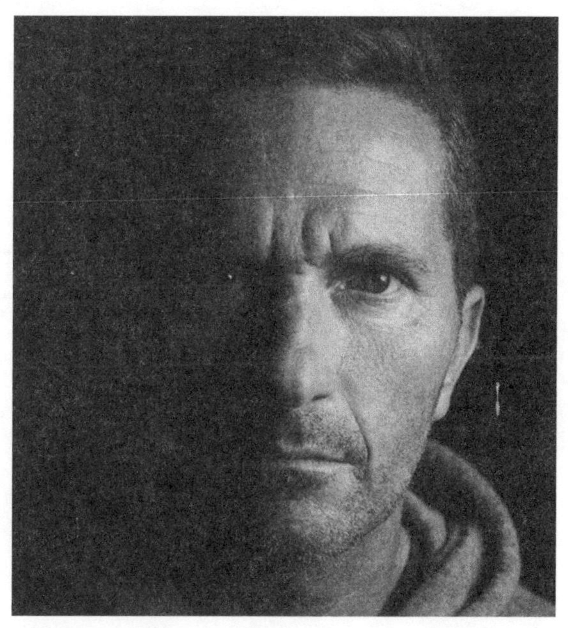

I take the good with the bad, and there is way more good as long as I maintain my spiritual condition. My relationship with God is paramount and without it I am nothing.

The amazing photographer Todd Glaser took this photo. It is one of my favorites. I was in Hawaii decompressing after a very tough time.

I hadn't showered in three days other than jumping in the ocean. I had just watched the sunset and spent most of that day alone in quiet contemplation.

No mask, no filter, no performance.

Just me.

Some days it's a battle. It takes every bit of strength just to look up at my waitress and order food. I wake up 2, 3, 4 times a night riddled with anxiety and fear.

I feel too much.

Some days it feels like everything is falling apart and nothing will work out. But then somehow, ultimately, it always does.

Money helps a lot and can be quite a panacea. Going online and buying a new Reigning Champ hoodie or walking into a Buck Mason store and buying anything they make feels so fantastic.

Taking friends to Bel Campo never fails to not only be the greatest meal ever, but also leaves me feeling like I've come a long way.

I don't know how it all gets done, but it does. It all seems impossible. I don't really know how to do anything, but I have these ideas...I have a vision or an idea for plans and then I put people in the right place, I hire people, and things get done.

It's so beautiful when it all comes together. A lot of times it seems like it's never going to get done or work out, then it comes out so much more beautifully than I ever could've imagined.

And sometimes it doesn't.

And that's okay, too.

FINAL THOUGHTS, PART 1

It's hard to wrap this up. I've jumped around a lot, I know. They say that books are never finished—they are simply abandoned.

So how do I walk away from this?

As I write this I'm in New York City. 62 Wooster in Soho, to be exact. I'm on the rooftop deck of the penthouse sunning myself and speaking into my iPhone as Siri types. It's 11:30 in the morning, and it couldn't be any more beautiful.

In fact, this may be the most beautiful day that has ever existed. It's exactly 70° and there is not a cloud in the sky. I feel so incredibly comfortable and calm as the morning sun gently warms my bare skin. I feel a great sense of accomplishment for finishing this book.

I'm not a writer.

Camus is a writer.

Paulo Coelho is a writer.

If even one person reads this and finds meaning and usefulness in it, then I've done a good job.

I'm just a normal guy from a small town in the Midwest who made a complete fucking mess of my life. By the grace of God, 17 years ago I got sober, and to the best of my ability—one day at a time—I have never taken that for granted.

Recovery from alcoholism and addiction is so rare, even more so if you factor in all of the other marks I had against me:

Immigrant parents, abuse, neglect, learning disabilities, and for the most part a pretty horrific childhood.

I can't spell or type and as far as education I don't even have a high school diploma.

I'm also a convicted felon.

Throw all of that together, and my chances of survival were pretty grim.

But here I am as a testament to the grace and power of a living, loving God and an example of what any of us can do if we simply put our minds to it. I've said it before and I'll say it again because it bears repeating:

If an idiot like me, with every possible mark against me and so many obstacles in my way, can make it...that is all the proof you will ever need that you can do, and be, and experience absolutely positively anything you want!

Please, please, please. Right here, right now, take pen to paper. I have provided the space for you on the last pages of this book. Please write down with as much detail as you can muster your one-year, three-year, and five-year plan.

Be specific.

Be realistic.

But at the same time, allow yourself to dream.

In fact, you know what...fuck it.

Don't be realistic.

My crazy ass dreams of things far beyond reality and those plans have not only come to fruition, they've exploded in a much bigger and more profound way than I could imagine.

Do not listen to the voice in your head, listen to the voice in your heart.

Remember you are the author of your book of life.

You are the director.

You are the producer.

You are the star.

We were created in God's image and each and every one of us is an incredibly unique, beautiful and powerful particle of God, and it is our birthright to create and express God's love and power and glory! I sincerely wish you the best that life has to offer because you deserve it!

May God bless you and keep you!

FINAL THOUGHTS, PART 2

There's so much more I want to say. Partly because I have much more in me, and partly because I'm scared this book is no good.

Jeremy, the young man who helps me write because I cannot spell or type or put things into any sort of cohesive format, recently paraphrased Paul Valéry to me: "A book is never finished, only abandoned."

Well, I am now for the 19th and final time abandoning this book. But I will leave you with this quote by Bjork because it really concisely explains what I've babbled on about for more pages than I should have:

"...after tragedies one has to invent a new world, knit it or embroider, make it up. It's not gonna be given to you because you deserve it, it doesn't work that way. You have to imagine something that doesn't exist and dig a cave into the future and demand space. It's a territorial hope affair. At the time, that digging is utopian but in the future it will become your reality."

KHALIL RAFATI is a high school dropout, convicted felon, and former heroin and crack addict.

Now he is a speaker, author, and health and wellness entrepreneur. He is the founder and owner of Malibu Beach Yoga and SunLife Organics, a rapidly growing chain of health food cafés with locations in California, Texas, and Arizona.

He also founded Riviera Recovery, a transitional living facility for drug addicts and alcoholics, is a board member of the Tashi Lhunpo Monastery, and through his incredible relationship with Khensur Rinpoche Lobzang Tsetan he is on the board of the Siddhartha School Project.